Linda Ronstadt

An illustrated biography by CONNIE BERMAN

PROTEUS

PROTEUS BOOKS is an imprint of
The Proteus Publishing Group

United Kingdom
PROTEUS (PUBLISHING) LIMITED
Bremar House,
Sale Place,
London, W2 1PT.

United States
PROTEUS PUBLISHING COMPANY
304, East John Street,
Carson City,
Nevada.

ISBN 0 906071 08 9

First published in US. April 1980
© 1980 by Connie Berman
All rights reserved.

Typeset in Scotland by
Computacomp (UK) Ltd.,
and printed and bound
in Hong Kong by
South China Printing Co.

... wistful ...

expert tutelage. Linda is no passive puppet, engineered by some sophisticated background machinery. She is a very seductive and thoughtful personality, wooing the audience as much with her sensuality and her consummate humanness and openness of emotion as that terrific range of voice. Linda Ronstadt is one performer who has not established a separate and fabricated onstage personality. When Linda sings, the feeling is real and when she mourns lost love and plaintively tells of low-down aches and psychic pain, you know that those are abysses that Linda has struggled through herself. Suffering, and being bruised are a large part of the musical themes in Linda's repertoire and they are very real.

Her popularity has definitely been heightened because of her vast sex appeal. Other singers may be prettier, others may be better endowed physically, but Linda has a highly combustive combination of vamp and innocent, a kind of wanton ingenuousness that the late Marilyn Monroe conveyed.

Much of rock music, after all, and especially most of the brand that Linda sings, is about love and sex, and the aching quality that she projects, the heady rush of lust that she belts out, is all very close to the

surface. While other female singers have been withdrawn and tentative and even a little antiseptic in their sexuality, Linda lets it all hang out. Not even Dolly Parton, with that exaggerated hourglass figure could compare to Linda, as winning and seductive as she is, when she pounces onstage in cut-off jeans and a close-fitting shirt, her brown eyes limpid with emotion. She's well aware of her sexual quotient but it's also something she feels remarkably ambivalent about. One moment she's posing in a slip for an album cover; the next minute she grouses that people just regard her as a piece of cheese.

But the ambivalence has been only part of the kaleidoscopic nature that is Linda Ronstadt, where emotions and feelings are constantly churning. Linda's life has been one fraught with confusion, mistakes, a lot of angst and pain. It hasn't been any easy, cocooned existence since she left Tucson to make it in California. And the ups and downs have been reflected in her music, which more than anything else is a barometer to how Linda feels at the moment.

All in all, Linda is an interesting and captivating lady, both before the microphone and on the stage. It's not her talent alone that woos her so many fans, but the real drama of her life that has been played out in her songs. Depressed, elated, guilt-ridden, tormented, giddy, Linda's been through the emotional turbulence that she's just really working out now. Linda relates so well because she seems one of us, not some rarified goddess separate from the trials and tribulations of everyday life. It's her hurting quality in fact that makes her all the more popular. We know that if she's made it through rough times, there is hope for us.

Like other major figures in rock and pop, like the Beatles and Elvis Presley, Linda has been an influential and strong force in music. She's made the softer sound more popular, helping audiences shift away from the hard, metallic, acid rock sounds of the late 60's. And, moreover, through Linda, the age of the girl singer has been realized and come into flower.

Along the way to supreme success, she's adorned a host of magazine covers, like Time, Us, People; sang for President Carter and won nearly every award in the rock, pop and country awards categories that she could possibly qualify for. The little girl who came out to Los Angeles a novice is now enjoying more success than she ever dreamed of. She has become the musical mascot for millions of radio, record and television listeners.

And she's still changing all the time—from little girl lost to worldly vamp to casual, relaxed cowgirl to smart, articulate spokeswoman, to

"In the first grade," Linda Ronstadt remembers, "I always thought it didn't matter if I learned to add because I wouldn't have to when I was a singer. I kept at singing because I had no back door. I had burned my bridges. I couldn't add."

Linda Marie Ronstadt was born on July 15, 1946, in Tucson, Arizona, and soon after she learned to talk, music became an abiding passion with her. She came from a musical family and the strains of the blaring radio and her father's syncopated strumming on the guitar filled her early days. As a toddler, she would curl up on the floor with her ear pressed close to the radio, rocking even as a child to the sounds and rhythms of the Mexican music that was played.

"I discovered how to turn on the radio when I was about three years old, and then it was all over for me," she remembers.

"I was just so into music. My father was a singer and it was just the neatest thing. I loved it. The first thing I can remember when I was a kid

was just begging my father to play the guitar. I used to pester him to death."

Linda has dubbed herself a "radio kid," one whose world during her childhood years was so full of the varied music on the radio. Since the place was Arizona, the Southwest which still smacked of pioneer life in many ways, most of the stations played country tunes or else ethnic songs that were popular in the area—Linda called them "funky Mexican stations." She would listen to the tunes and sing along, trying to imitate with her young and raw voice the heavy sensuality of the female Mexican singers, with their "ranchera"-styled tunes.

In the blistering and searing hot summer months in Tucson, people stayed indoors as much as they could and did quiet, peaceful things to deal with the heat. Linda would lie on the cement floor, absorbing its soothing coolness as the temperatures soared around her, and press her cheek to the radio to listen to the songs. "I had grooves on my cheeks," she recalls with a laugh.

Before she was in her teens, Linda knew every note and lyric of the hip-swaggering Elvis Presley songs that throbbed on the radio. But she also liked the sounds of such disparate artists as the Beach Boys, Peggy Lee, Billie Holiday, Hank Williams, Ray Charles, Sam Cooke, George Jones and Tammy Wynette. And she learned to appreciate the gossamer, high-voiced sounds of Joan Baez.

"I used to sing along with Joan Baez records—I thought I had a voice just like hers. Then I found out. The first moment you listen to yourself, it takes time to get used to that sound. It might be valid, even good, but you don't have a taste for it. ... There weren't that many girls in Tucson who could sing that well, I guess. I just fooled myself."

Linda responded to the kind of music, whatever its brand, with a strong beat and sound and throbbing soul. No quiet, simple, soft mood music for her. She much preferred the singers who belted out their songs and enjoyed the lusty, hard-driving potency of rock and roll.

Her father, Gilbert, who owned a hardware store in Tucson—called Ronstadt's Hardware Store—was largely responsible for cultivating Linda's taste in music. He was a colorful personality with an interesting blend of Mexican, German and English backgrounds in his heritage. He loved the catchy Mexican songs and found an eager and rapt audience in Linda as he would sit on the living room couch on lazy Sunday afternoons and play his guitar. Occasionally he would team up with some of the mariachi bands in the area and provide his services as singer and guitarist.

Linda's family background is a curious mixture of country roots people

with a more sophisticated and rarified strain. Her father's family was very much into the land. Linda's grandfather worked as a rancher in Arizona. And his father, Linda's great-grandfather on the paternal side, was the

first mining engineer in the northern part of Mexico and also served in the Mexican army. He had come over to Mexico after his birth in Germany.

In addition to Linda's grandfather's interest in ranching, he operated a modest wagon-making shop that eventually, with the coming of more modern times, evolved into a hardware store right in Tucson. So Linda's father was involved right from the start in both the ranch and the hardware businesses.

But however great his aptitude in business, Gilbert Ronstadt's heart really was in making music. He is a most talented singer with a lustrous and rich and slow vibrato voice that ranges from the depths of baritone to the height of tenor notes. Linda once described it as a voice "full of honey and thick."

As a young man in his twenties, Gilbert Ronstadt had sung professionally on a radio show and played for various club and party functions from time to time. But his family were fully cognizant of their emigration from the Old World to the New, mostly to make a better life and a good living. That meant they did not think that show business was a suitable way of life for a man who wanted to become someone. So, despite his enchantment with singing, Gilbert regarded it as a hobby and settled down to the more practical tasks of hardware and ranching.

Linda's mother was a well-connected society lady from Michigan. She stresses that her mother was not snobby, just dutiful as those well-connected people feel they must be. Her mother was a member of one of the prestigious sororities at an Arizona college when Gilbert Ronstadt swept her off her well-heeled and expensively shod feet. Back in her genteel hometown of Michigan, Linda's mother had never seen anything like this dashing, kind of daredevil cowboy who wooed Linda by riding his horse right up the steps of her sorority house to ask her out. He was a handsome, dark-haired cavalier of a man, with a penchant for adventure. But he was also determined and solid and the intriguing combination was enough to make Linda's mother, with her staid Daughters of the American Revolution type background, fall in love. It was a case of the Mexican-bred cowboy winning the heart of the more pristine, sheltered society girl. Linda's personality and singing style today reflects that dual influence of the sophisticate and the ranch hand.

Linda's mother, still strong and intelligent and a vital woman, is the daughter of a scientifically gifted inventor named Lloyd Copeland. He invented an electric stove and a kind of early microwave oven. Her mother's family bore a mixed heritage of German, English and Dutch.

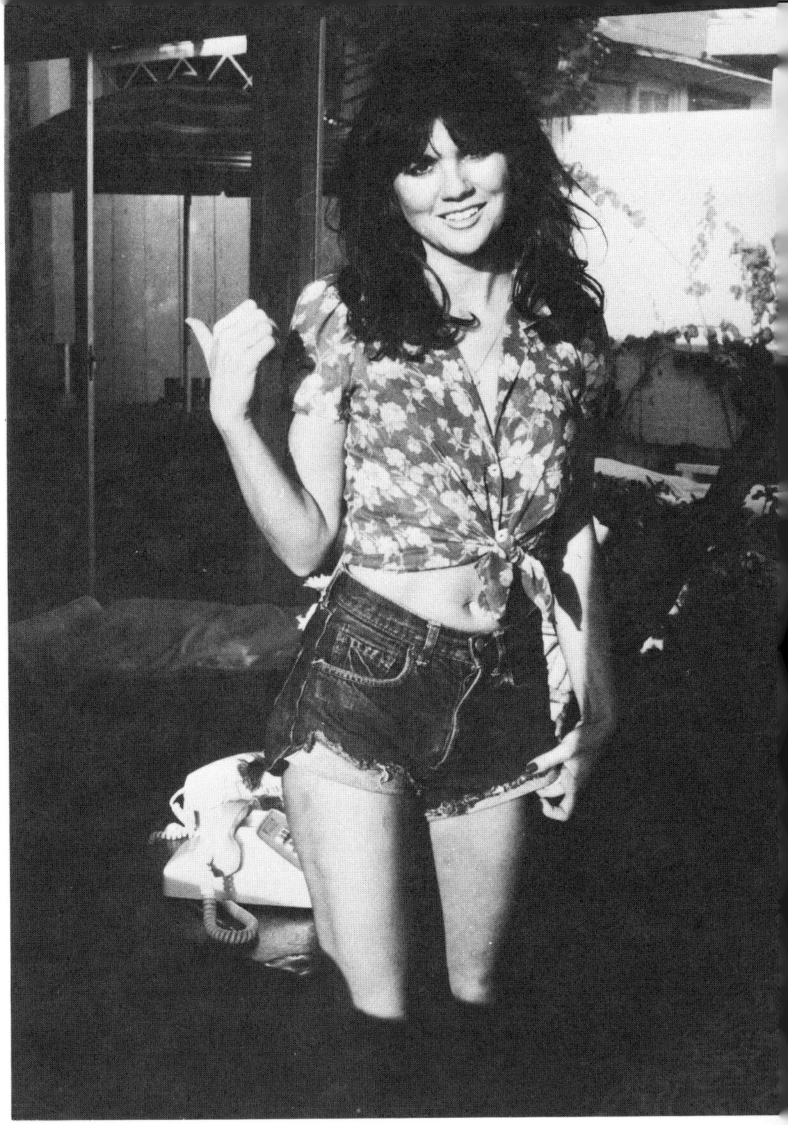

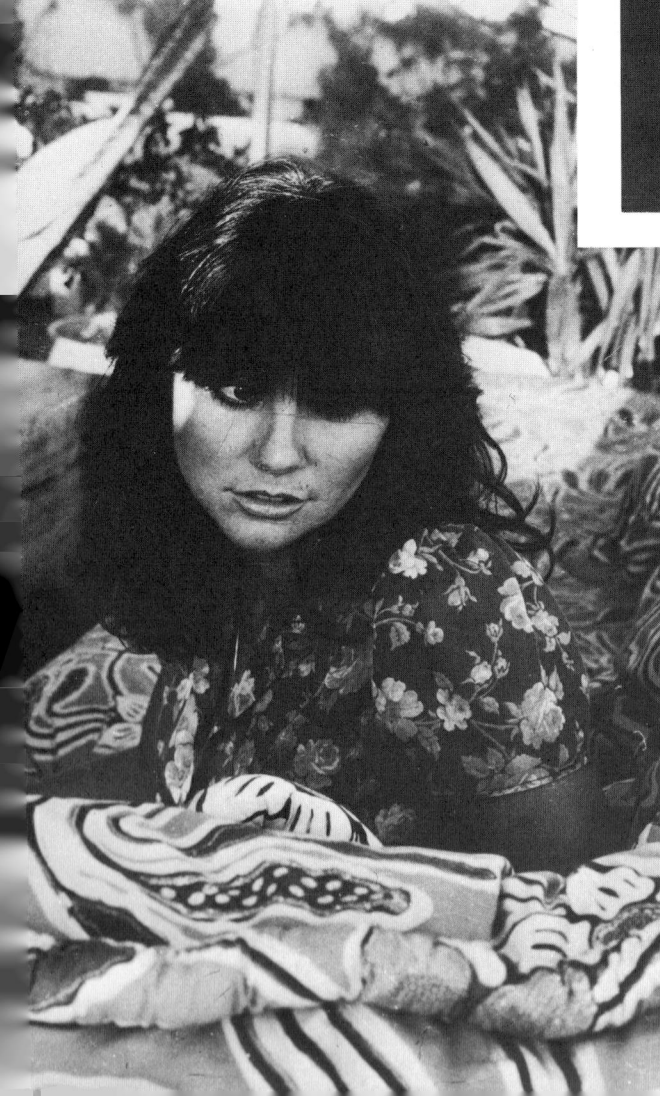

Relaxing at home on Malibu Beach

Linda did not have one of those rags-to-riches, gritty upbringings. She did not have to suffer materially because of lack of money like her close friend Dolly Parton. Indeed, the Ronstadt family was quite prosperous as her father's business fared well. Linda owned a pony and then a horse as a child. This iconoclastic, torchy rock queen who scampers around stage in revealing blouses and hot pants and loves to talk about sex, was once a demure debutante for a season in Tucson, in accordance with her mother's wishes.

Her recollections of her childhood seem to be happy and solid ones, not marred by any great tragedies or any overwhelming psychological problems. She talks enthusiastically today about her family and speaks fondly of the times they spent together singing.

Linda and her father would sing along with her sister and two brothers. Linda says her older brother had a wonderfully rich soprano voice and that he really had the most vocal talent of anyone in the family. Linda loved to listen to him sing and tried to emulate his style. She recalls that he was the one she wanted to copy as his voice soared up to the high notes as he performed in the Tucson Boys Choir. "He had a glorious soprano," Linda compliments.

One day Linda's sister was playing a song at the piano and her brother was singing along, his golden soprano gliding easily over the notes as his sister played. Linda, only four at the time, promptly announced that she wanted to sing too, then started to sing. She displayed an amazingly clear vibrato and her sister, obviously impressed, said to their brother, "I think we have a soprano here."

Linda would harmonize with her brother and sister and her father, although she playfully complains that her father, despite his natural gifts, has the worst time of all. Linda says his slow-moving tempo is because he doesn't play with a band.

During this informal, impromptu harmonizing, Linda sang the high notes of a soprano. But then when she was 14, she discovered that she had quite another, different voice. Her brother and sister were performing a duet called "The Stockade Blues," which was made popular by Peter, Paul and Mary.

As Linda describes what happened, "I came walking around the corner and I just threw in the high harmony. I did it in my chest voice and I surprised myself. When I started out with my chest voice, I could only sing straight, with no vibrato."

It was soon after Linda found her so-called chest voice, the one that she uses today, that she started singing professionally with her brother and

sister. They called themselves The Three Ronstadts and did commercial background singing, a little bluegrass, and some folk music, and a few Mexican tunes. They hardly overwhelmed their audiences, however. The Three Ronstadts never seemed slated for any great stardom and did not attract the notice of any important talent scouts.

Linda confesses that she always considered herself a singer, even before she did any professional work, even before she left college to perform with a rock band. "I'm a singer, that's what I do," she would proclaim to people. She never stopped to decide whether she was any good or not, or whether she was good enough to make it. She had just decided that that was what she was going to be and nothing would prevent her from that aim. Ingenuously, she believed that all she had to do was cut a record and then she would become a success.

Part of the reason Linda focused so intently on music was that she hated school. It varied from being a bore to her to being more of a trauma. Not one to be readily engrossed with book learning, Linda found herself seething with rebellion which reached a peak during her teenage years.

She attended a series of Catholic schools which was another reason she found education such an unsavory experience. She didn't get along well with the nuns, who, she recalls with a grimace, hated her because of her preoccupation with boys.

"Those nuns still make me uptight," she says. "I never learned anything in school. Fortunately my father taught me to read at home but I still can't add. I had to jump into what I wanted to do right away."

School today still provokes bitter, unpleasant memories for her. "School became irrelevant, so my choices were to sing or maybe get a job in a hotel as a waitress. I don't know how to do anything else.

"I feel very cheated by the system in general. I went to Catholic schools, which made me think that all schools are useless. All I learned was how to go to sleep in class. So I don't have a high school diploma."

The nuns, Linda explains, sternly disapproved of her precocious and wild ways. Like a budding Lolita, young Linda wore a lot of lipstick, dressed in sexy clothes and painted her nails with fire engine red nail polish. "I came on too strong," she says. "I still do."

She was also an incorrigible flirt and a tease, even when it was vastly inappropriate. Linda was just a born seductress. She tells of one incident which involved a young priest who had just been ordained in catechism class. Linda and her friends would write the answers to the catechism high up on their legs. When the teacher would give them tests, they would

provocatively slide their dresses up and expose suggestive parts of skin, in order to copy down the answers. The priest would turn away quickly, blushing with embarrassment. Linda remembers the incident with one part sheepishness about her naughtiness and one part pride in the effects of her flirtatiousness.

While Linda was struggling with the heat wave of adolescent sexuality that would never be tamed, she was also struggling with a goal that was unique in her milieu. Most of her peers had no intentions of embarking

3

When Linda picked up and headed for Los Angeles in 1964, it was an exciting time for musicians to create their innovative sounds out there. Los Angeles was then emerging as the dominant center for rock music, the place where all the dissonant and disparate rock-wave sounds were being made. The eager participants in the L.A. music scene believed that rock was power, that it alone had the strength to carry forth the messages they, the youth, wanted the world to hear. Rock was their communication medium; it alone could convey the power they sought, the energy they had that was bouncing around inside waiting to be unleashed. Whether the songs were protests of government policy, laments for unrequited love, or simply blazing, blistering sexual calls, they were best shown off in the rock mode.

Clusters of rock musicians formed small, informal colonies around the Los Angeles section of Echo Park, Laurel Canyon and Venice. Aspiring

singers and guitarists and drummers flocked to these spots, where such impressive figures as Jackson Browne and Bonnie Raitt presided. This was the place where two men named Don Henley and Glenn Frey met up with each other and formed the nucleus of a group that was to later become famous as the Eagles. Neil Young, Joni Mitchell and Stephen Stills nestled in homes around Laurel Canyon, with Frank Zappa just footsteps away. Jim Morrison of the Doors would sleep on the beach and visit his friends' houses when he woke up. These leaders of the rock music movement were coming together, fomenting their ideas and their musical signatures as the heavy and explosive rock music emerged.

Linda had stationed herself in an apartment in Ocean Park, where she found the whole explosiveness of the movement very exciting and stimulating. It was a far more expansive experience than the sheltered milieu of Tucson. "We were all learning about drugs, philosophy and music," Linda recalls.

She got in touch with a fellow Arizonan named Bob Kimmel, who played rhythm guitar. Together they mulled over the possibility of forming a band and contacted a lead guitarist named Kenny Edwards. The threesome decided to call themselves The Stone Poneys, named after the Charlie Patton song called *Stone Poney Blues*. The threesome wanted to make their contribution to the musical energy that was swelling in the Los Angeles area.

The Stone Poneys never quite jelled as a rock act. Linda today describes their efforts as "crude," and it's clear that they suffered from what could be called a terminal case of floundering—in search of a definite style and approach.

Linda was full of the country sounds that she'd learned out in Arizona but those weren't the music of the moment in California. She would talk about country music and the group would look at her quizzically. So The Stone Poneys assumed a folk-rock stance.

"We started off as an acoustic rock band," she says, "and played clubs like the Insomniac and a lot of beer pads. Places like that. We had some good times and some bad times, but we were always breaking up. We were always playing in opposite musical directions."

"The Stone Poneys," Linda sums up, "tried to combine the roots with rock and roll and we were miserable."

But, rough and fuzzy as their music was, the Stone Poneys did manage to perform at the Troubadour which was the place which showed you had amounted to something in the rock world to land an engagement.

The Troubadour was the focal point of all the jamming musical force

Linda is a perfectionist and works hard to get a new song just right.

in Los Angeles. It was a shabby, somewhat dilapidated bar filled not only with rock fans but also fast-talking, would-be record company executives and aspiring musicians who hoped to figure out what was selling that week and then cash in. It was a showcase that attracted people of prestigious reputations who could have performed in more impressive places, but this, modest as it was, was the West Coast mecca for the cognoscenti of the music world. It was the "in" place to be and to perform. It had the atmosphere of a private club and the acts who got up on stage to perform were hopeful that some of the big names, performers as well as executives in the audience, might mention their names and garner them a recording contract. Rock groups felt that they hadn't really made it big unless they played at the Troub, as it was fondly called by those who knew its reputations well. Playing there could make a faltering, stagnant career take off overnight if the right people noticed and were impressed. Hot, tacky, packed and unluxurious as it was, the Troubadour was an important place.

And, true to form, it was the Poneys, two-week stint there which landed them their first recording contract, with Capitol Records.

Professionally, the Stone Poneys gave a group impression that was clumsy, but Linda, with her raw and powerful voice and her instinct for phrasing, shone out above the others in performances. Billboard, after reviewing a Stone Poney concert in 1968, warned auspiciously, "Watch out for Linda Ronstadt." They further promised that Linda would become one of the nation's top vocalists.

The Stone Poneys became mildly successful, in a kind of tepid way that many rock groups do. In other words they made money and played club dates but they never became the kind of monster act that commands the top halls and prices and makes an indelible notch in the music industry. They played a lot of the local clubs in the Los Angeles area fairly regularly and made three fairly mediocre albums. They toured and appeared in such clubs as Cafe a Go Go in New York and Club 47 of Boston. Record executives were somewhat impressed by the Stone Poneys but wanted to mold them in a different vein. They thought the group would be better off if they called themselves The Signets and did surfing music like the Beach Boys.

On the notes of their first album, Jerry Hopkins wrote, "a lovely bouquet of musical flowers and wheat, the beauty and staff of life."

In her role as lead singer in the 1960's, Linda occupied a lone position except perhaps for Grace Slick of Jefferson Airplane, which would later become Jefferson Starship. In those days, lead singers were men. But it

was her flamboyant, torchy belting that gave the Stone Poneys their first hit—*Different Drum*. Released in 1967, shortly before the group disbanded, *Different Drum* was an ode to lost love and breaking up. The song climbed rapidly up the charts and made Linda a star in her own right. She was singled out for praise and the group's next album was significantly called Linda Ronstadt—Stone Poneys and Friends.

But despite the heady attention, Linda did not find it easy to have a hit record. Success brought trauma of its own.

"Having a hit record when I was 21 made me real visible to the music

community and I didn't feel I was ready for that examination. I wasn't very good and it made me real embarrassed. I felt people in the business resented me. I still struggle with that."

But with *Different Drum*, back in 1967, which was written by one of the Monkees, Mike Nesmith, Linda was also struggling to hold the group together. They toured after their hit as a warm-up act for the Doors, which Linda recalls, pulling no punches, as an experience that was the pits. But the trio just couldn't synthesize their music coherently and in 1968, they disbanded, and Linda was left as a solo to fulfill the Stone Poneys record contract with Capitol.

She was scared to death at the prospect of being a solo act. Being up there on the stage by herself terrified her and shook her already quavering self-esteem. Linda felt insecure about her singing ability and frightened without some men to assist her in performances.

"I was so intimidated by the quality of everybody's musicianship that instead of trying to be better, I chickened out and wouldn't work."

As much as Linda today projects an image of brazen self-confidence as a woman, back then she was admittedly crippled by fear. "It took me four years to get to the point where I could get on stage as a single. At first I just couldn't open my mouth on stage. I was so shy."

The shyness may have been hindering, but Linda began gaining ground as an artist. She made her bow as a single at the popular Whiskey a Go Go Club in Los Angeles, in March, 1969, and displayed a fine audience rapport. Although one reviewer complained that she had a tendency to get too high-pitched at times, he nevertheless complimented that she obviously put everything she could into her songs and remarked on her wide vocal range, "from high-pitched soprano to throaty guttural slurs."

She was backed by a variety of groups and perhaps the impermanence of Linda's bands says more about her own feelings of confusion musically at this time. She had the talent and the vocal capacity, but she was emotionally hampered and she suffered from lack of good guidance. For a period, she was backed by a group that went on to achieve enormous success on its own as the Eagles, and by another band called Swamp Water.

What she became was a cult artist, bereft of any real national or pop stature, but a singer recognized by people who knew something about music. She was a favorite among the frequenters of the Los Angeles and San Francisco club scene and a favorite among the rock musicians themselves. But as far as emerging as the powerful artist she could be,

based on her stage presence and her voice, Linda was in a nether world. She made what she disparagingly refers to as "indifferent albums" and sang at nondescript clubs and hung out with other musicians. But her career wasn't taking off the way some reviewers predicted it would.

Linda evaluates that time now as being so hazy because she simply didn't know that much about singing. She had come to Los Angeles a neophyte, and despite her performances, had managed to stay that way. She arrived in California full of family praise but with no inkling of what it took to become a rock star. And the realities were hard, especially because Linda realized that there were a lot of people who weren't going to make it. And she was plagued with insecurities. "I was so unsure of myself. I was afraid to tell the musicians what to play or to assert myself in the management situation. I have a tendency to let other people shape me. If I'm going with someone and he gets at all critical of my music, the bottom falls out for me."

Linda tries a new number with Andrew Gold.

She was also recording on her own, working with session men not only in the West Coast, but also in Nashville and in Muscle Shoals to evoke that country flavor she is noted for. The compelling amalgam of the southern California sound with country soul was what was making Linda a unique commodity.

But she was hesitant about taking a leadership role with her band. She had to give them direction and often she just wanted to be one of the guys, fading away from the lead spotlight. As she lamented at one point during that difficult transition period from group member to successful solo, "I'd like to be in the band and just sing and play cowbell and tambourine. I'm tired of being a single and I'm tired of the hassles of being a girl."

The mantle of lady rock star was clearly not an easy one for Linda to shoulder. She found herself assuming the demeanor of a truck driver to bark out orders and get people to pay attention to her. Or else she switched roles and became a cutie-pie flirt, cozying up to men with a demure and sometimes not so demure wink of her eyes and get them to listen to her that way.

Linda often explains away the sluggish quality of her music during this time as a case of mixing business with pleasure. Her managers and producers usually were her boyfriends. Linda found herself playing the child to their daddy-type roles. Instead of relying on her own good instincts and capabilities, Linda listened to men, allowing herself to be manipulated by and dictated to by them. It didn't help that Linda was so good-looking and an outrageous flirt. She just couldn't contain that wild sexuality but it hampered her career then.

She was in desperate search of a mentor and a helping hand. And so she invariably wound up sleeping with the men who gave her advice. It was a terrible way to do career business, but Linda was so insecure that she didn't know how to do it any other way. Her professional relationships usually wound up becoming relationships in every sense of the word.

"And that is always a bad idea," she comments today. "First there is business, then business and sex, then the business goes sour and then there is no sex."

But she still was making some good music, although it wasn't consistently good. Despite her personal morass, the strength of her talent shone through. Her first solo album for Capitol was called *Hand Sown, Home Grown*. It was interesting but fairly sketchy. Her extraordinary vocal talents were displayed to advantage in the country standard, *Silver Threads*

4

2113335

In every major star's life there is usually one person who operates behind the scenes and has made all the difference in their career, who translated their raw, often unshaped talent into a major success. With Diana Ross, it was a shrewd and market-wise man named Berry Gordy, who founded Motown Records and helped groom the skinny black kid into a supreme talent. With Linda Ronstadt, it was Peter Asher who molded her from a cult artist who was respected by cognoscenti yet little known elsewhere, into an international star.

Peter Asher, formerly of the rock group called Peter And Gordon, is the man credited with the overall improvement in Linda's music and her records, which in turn led to her achieving a huge recognition quotient among listeners. Red-haired and bespectacled, Peter projects a sort of absent-minded professor image which couldn't be further from the truth. He is an extremely intelligent and shrewd manager and producer with a quick, analytical mind, swift to ferret out the unique charms of a

performer, and equally quick to market them in a way that will appeal to the public. Musically, Asher is very astute. Not only is he a producer who can accomplish and deliver, but he is also a producer who knows his music.

Asher, British-born, is not like your usual variety of recorder-producer-hyper-hustler. He doesn't have the kind of aggressive demeanor that is characteristic of most major producers in the records field.

He started off his career not in music but in acting, as a child star of sorts with his sister Jane—who then became famous as the girlfriend of Paul McCartney.

One of Asher's films was Outpost to Malaya, which he made with Claudette Colbert. He also did some stage work, and then meandered into the music field. It became an avid interest to him, so he polished up his guitar-playing enough so that in 1962, he became the Peter half of a duet named Peter and Gordon. The two achieved minor success with songs like *World Without Love*, written by McCartney and Lennon, and *Lady Godiva*, which was probably the duet's biggest hit.

But the group broke up in 1967, since Peter never found being onstage all that comfortable. He far preferred the backstage machination and the often subtle but important details in a performer's offering that made the difference between being a star and not being one.

When Peter was studying philosophy at London University he was also dabbling in his first record production. He joined Apple Records at Paul McCartney's behest to scout for new talent and discovered a young singer named James Taylor. Asher then left Apple to migrate to Los Angeles, where he took Taylor and worked with his sister Kate and Cat Stevens. But when Linda Ronstadt asked him to help her in her recording, Asher decided to hone down his stable and manage just two clients, which he still maintains today—Taylor and Linda. Despite requests from some of the biggest names in the business, Asher refuses to increase his quantity, preferring a specialized approach.

Right away, Asher soothed Linda's jangled nerves and concentrated on handling the troublesome business matters that prevented her from achieving her artistry. That is Asher's particular modus operandi with his people—he also produced James Taylor's records. He keeps his clients away from the worrisome details of crowds, bookings, the press, promoters and other concerns that keep a performer diverted from the main activity of his life—performing.

The vulturous way these details erode a performer's psyche is revealed by Linda when she says that, about Asher, "He keeps them from moving

At a reception in L.A. Linda and manager Peter Asher share a joke.

in on me like a herd of barracudas until there's no flesh left on my bones."

That Ronstadt hired Asher in the first place was a significant step in a good direction for her. She had become mature enough to realize that her professional relationship with men who became her lovers was damaging and stultifying to her career. Undoubtedly, one of the reasons Asher has been able to help Linda in her career and the reason she has responded so well to him is that there is absolutely no sex involved.

Ronstadt asked Asher to help her in 1973, when she was completing her album, *Don't Cry Now*. She was displeased and downright unhappy with the way the album was sounding, her confidence in her singing was practically nil and recording was a nightmare to her. She recalls being so depressed when she was making an album that she would fall asleep under the console with the monitors going full volume just to escape from her chores.

But Asher helped her with the album, which was a significant cut above her previous solo efforts. For the first time, Linda's voice was the focal point of the album, and not lost in some muddied interpretations and timing that didn't suit her. Her voice showed more power and more effectiveness. Linda was definitely singing better. And it seemed that for the first time she had figured out how to be emotional with her voice, the difference between lack of sentiment and mechanical delivery and a more from the heart way of appealing to the audience. In the past, her critics have accused her of having a great voice but showing little feeling. It was apparent that the tremendous vulnerability which she felt was not being translated and too threatening for her to convey to the stage.

After working just a few months under Asher's tutelage, Linda announced, in a more optimistic note, "I've finally learned how to sing. I used to watch people sit down and practice and work every day and they'd get better and I never would—but now that's different."

Although Asher only assisted with the production of *Don't Cry Now* at the end of its completion, it was the first of Linda's records to enjoy more than a moderate level of success. It was on the national charts for more than 45 weeks, a vigorous showing of an album by any standard. And the success of the album bred more confidence for Linda, and as she did better, her singing became better. She relaxed and became less frightened of the recording medium.

The slight hesitancy and guardedness that she showed with *Don't Cry Now* were dispelled by the time that Linda made *Heart Like A Wheel*, her first album completed totally under Asher's guidance. She found, for the first time, that recording could be a pleasurable experience, especially with Peter there to help her and deal with the bugbears. She was more confident, more self-assured going into the making of the album and that showed on the record. And the healthy faith in herself paid off. *Heart Like A Wheel* made number one on the album charts and also gave her two number one singles, *You're No Good*, and *I Can't Help It If I'm Still In Love With You*. Linda for the first time in her career became an authentic pop-rock star and not just a promising vocalist, a title that she held and wore grudgingly for years.

Asher says that as Linda's confidence increased, "she started singing better and when she started singing better, her confidence increased."

Undoubtedly, Asher has helped Linda get that confidence, because he is one of the first to remark on how excellent the quality of her voice is, how brilliant she is musically.

For her part, Linda's thankful that she finally divested herself of her

works harder now, but she's more secure, more eager to try again. There's more of a realistic pattern to her life and that makes Linda feel better.

As she explains, "I'm a mirror. A real reflective person, and in a way it's horrible because I'm always at the mercy of my surroundings.

"So I need a catalyst, always, and I need a good sounding board that I can trust. I hardly trust anybody, period, and I hardly trust anybody's taste. You have to find somebody that you know knows how to handle you, knows how to reinforce you without indulging or greasing you."

Working with Peter has been a very positive thing for Linda, and she explains their relationship in terms of a marriage. She admits that she can't imagine ever working with anyone else, because they both suit each other so perfectly. He understands, she explains, the myriad insecurities, her tardiness, her scattered approach. And she in turn understands when he becomes shy and insecure himself.

Having a good time on stage. Linda with guitarist Waddy Wachtel and (back to the camera) bassman Kenny Edwards.

But as her success with the help of Peter mounted, Linda found other problems. For example, she found it hard to deal with her newfound success, taking pain from it as much as she took failure. *Heart Like A Wheel* was her first album to reach number one and sell a million copies.

She felt apologetic about what was happening, unworthy of the attention and the success, and found herself walking around trying to explain away her achievement as if it was all a mistake. But gradually, with the aid of a psychiatrist who really turned her life around, Linda learned how to accept herself as a powerful rock figure.

"The problem is she doesn't know how to handle being famous," Asher once said. He may be right. When Linda had split from the Stone Poneys, she spent her days broke and singing at tawdry clubs, barefoot and braless, floundering for a style to call her own. "For a long time she wanted to buy a fancy car. Now that she can have her choice of cars, she doesn't know which one she wants."

So it was not merely a matter of dealing with success, and achieving it

5

She wails. She moans. She belts. She roars. Linda Ronstadt uses that fantastic, rich and sensual voice of hers like an instrument. She can be loud and raucous and bellowing; she can be soft and demure and falsetto. At once, her voice can display an encyclopedic range of emotions—nostalgia imbued with grief, heartbreak tinged with bitterness, contrariness laced with command. What is astonishing about the music of Linda Ronstadt is not only that she has one of the richest and most gifted ranges of voice in the country, if not the world. But also, perhaps more important than the raw material quotient, Linda expresses so much in her singing—the natural gifts are doubly enhanced by the emotion that she seems to wrench and wring out of every pore.

This supreme expressiveness is a relatively new quality. It's something that she learned to do as she became more confident—to reveal the tremendous vulnerability she feels. Before, her singing was good, but more mechanical, more rote in quality. Now with Linda, the music you

hear and the singer you see is what you get—it's no glitzy act, no extravagant put-on where the facade melts away as soon as she leaves the stage. As she says, about this lack of a fabricated stage persona, "I'm never a different person offstage than I am onstage. I don't have a stage personality."

But that very lack of artifice, the realness about Linda Ronstadt that a listener senses when she croons about her psychic hurts and bruises is the major source of her popularity. Watching Linda sing is a little like peeking into another person's soul—because that's what Linda gives you.

So undisguised is Linda, so much is she a part of what she sings about, that she refuses to sing anything that she can't relate to, that doesn't evolve from her own experience. She says she can only sing about the emotions that she has and those emotions are very close to the surface. Nothing, she insists, that she sings is out of character, nor is it false.

There have been occasional and unfair stories that Peter Asher completely dictates what Linda performs. This is obviously not true; what happens is that Linda usually picks the tunes and she and Peter work on a setting for them. And he figures out a system to make the setting work and be integrated with the song.

How does Linda select her material? She explains that the process is usually triggered by something that happens in her own life and makes her respond in a visceral way to a song. She feels that the songs she sings have to be personal statements and say something about how she feels. Sometimes, even the finest songs that Peter Asher suggests to her won't work. For example, Asher heard an Elvis Costello record that would be a big hit, he thought, for Linda. But when Linda heard it, she couldn't figure out how to do the song because she couldn't relate to it personally.

"Though the melody has to match up with what I can do, the lyrics are the main thing," she says. "I look for something that feels like it is about me. Just like a songwriter will write a song that is about some feeling he just went through. I can't really sing a song that doesn't express my feelings in some way."

Linda similarly refused to sing Carole King's standard, *You've Got A Friend*. She explained her action at the time by saying that she didn't think she was anybody's friend. And she also turned down *I Don't Know How To Love Him* because the idea of singing that every night on stage was not what she wanted to do.

Linda's voice is hard to classify—it is not pure anything but a compelling meld of country, rock and blue grass with a light touch of folk. But the biggest element is country, the kind of pure, unadulterated

*Linda's boy scout outfit has become
one of her stage trademarks.*

Linda and Emmy Lou Harris join forces on a country classic.

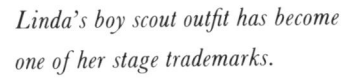

With Linda, it's just the opposite.

Her style of performing used to be more subdued in concert. But as Linda has been encouraged and coaxed out of her insecurities and fears, she has developed a much looser performing style. She used to assume a more stationary position and remain fixed in place, singing on almost a mechanical level. But now Linda, dressed in one of her boy scout outfits or a camisole top with high heels and short shorts will show more exuberance on stage. She used to keep those barefoot feet firmly planted on the ground, but now she's more likely to kick, to cavort, to run around the stage. Linda does love to sing and that love of singing has gradually, although not completely, conquered her fear of performing. She gives more of herself in concert than she used to.

Unlike many other singers and rock stars, Linda does not write any of her own material. She has collaborated on two songs, but she refuses to think of herself as a potential songwriter. She says that, "I'm not a songwriter and never will be, but there's no harm in trying to come up with something and throwing it on the wall to see if it sticks."

The two songs she wrote were featured on her *Hasten Down the Wind* album—one called *Try Me Again* which she felt was so personal it almost embarrassed her to sing it, and another called *Lo Sienta Mi Vida* which she says she wrote with her father and Stone Poney Kenny Edwards. But Linda envisions herself as an interpreter rather than a writer and claims that she would rather rely on the material of others.

"Some people sit down every day and they write, but I don't do that. I have a few ideas cooking, but my goal in life is not to be a songwriter. The fact that I wrote a song was like an added bonus in my life. But something pretty intense has to happen and it's got to be something I can write about in pretty specific terms. That whole combination of events has to happen in order for me to write a song. I just don't have the kind of craftsmanship that a writer would have to have to construct things out of every day experiences, in a way that makes it real interesting. I mean Paul Simon is the most gifted at that. He can write songs outside of his own experience so eloquently."

Her refusal to consider songwriting seriously may be a real intense commitment toward her universality as a singer. Linda is the one popular singer who seems to ably handle all diverse kinds of material—whether they be rhythm and blues or country and white gospel. It's also part of her stance as interpreter rather than leader. She insists, after all these years of lead singing, "I'd rather sing harmony than anything else. I really hate being a single artist. I don't like singing alone. If I can't get in a

focus, even with the assistance of Peter Asher near the completion of it. But at least *Don't Cry Now* was more promising and delivered more of the Ronstadt talent than before.

Don't Cry Now revealed that Linda could convey many moods in her singing. She could etch the messages of Randy Newman's piquant words as well as she could whallop out the rock sounds of the Eagles. On this album there was another stronger, more rock-hued version of *Silver Threads and Golden Needles*, as well as a stunning rendition of *Colorado* and *I Believe in You*. The improved version of *Silver Threads* was an index of Linda's own growth; she had finally learned to wield her voice more effectively.

But her albums were still disappointingly inconsistent. Some tracks would be outstanding and then others would just not measure up. As her confidence seemed to swell and ebb, so went the music. There was no one direction assumed, but many conflicting ones apparent.

But *Don't Cry Now*, as out of focus as it was, still marked a major change in Linda's musical career. Sales-wise it made an impression since it made the charts and showed a considerable profit, all of which increased Linda's confidence. And she capitalized on her success by stepping up her concert schedule and touring more than before. It was the album that showed that Linda was finally on the verge of something better.

But the splash finally came with *Heart Like A Wheel*, released in 1974 and her fifth solo album. *Heart Like A Wheel* was acclaimed as a triumph, and for the first time in Linda's life she was enjoying a super-charged hit album that was a true showcase of her talents. The album was made on the Capitol label, because she had to fulfill a prior commitment. It was called one of the best albums of country blended with rock by many reviewers. And Linda, at last, showed the kind of control and command of her material and voice that had eluded her for so many years. For the first time, her quality level was uniformly excellent and many chart-making songs spun off from the album, especially the taunting, teasing, chiding, *You're No Good*, which became her first number one single since *Different Drum*.

Heart Like A Wheel featured a collection of poignant and utterly captivating material that was vocally appealing by such gifted songwriters as Paul Anka, Hank Williams, Lowell George and John David Souther. Each song was obviously chosen with care and aptly suited to Linda's great talents. Unlike her previous albums which were uneven in content, each song fitted Linda musically like a glove. The result was first-rate and not the usual fair-to-middling rendition she usually found. For the first

time, her voice showed the grace, control and versatility that was always there but not always apparent.

Besides the inspired combination of song and artist, another element of Linda's success with *Heart Like A Wheel* was her backing musicians. Asher apparently spared no expense in hiring the finest people available such as Glen Frey, Herb Pederson, Don Henley, Chris Ethridge and Sneaky Pete Kleinow. Then there was a fine and capable group of background vocalists to enhance the music. Again, Asher's mastery and savvy came into play, as each background vocal was delivered by someone who was expertly equipped to handle it. This kind of technical excellence, instead of the often-muddled approach, showed Linda's tracks best off to advantage. When she sang, *I Can't Help It If I'm In Love With You*, the harmony vocal was executed by Emmylou Harris. The song was performed in a country vein, with guitar and fiddle accompaniment by Sneaky Pete and David Landley. Emmylou, at the time *Heart Like A Wheel* was released, had gained a considerable reputation as a provider of excellent backgrounds for Gram Parsons' albums. Other performers who added in the backgrounds were Peter Asher himself, Clydie King, Wendy Waldman, Maria Muldaur, Cissy Houston, Souther and Linda herself.

Other popular songs on the album included James Taylor's *You Can Close Your Eyes* and a hit by the later Buddy Holly called *It Doesn't Matter*. Linda was to discover that the early thumping and vigorous rock and roll tunes by the late gifted Holly were well suited to her voice, allowing it to display the active exuberance she's famous for.

The opening cut, written by Clint Ballard Jr. and previously recorded as a rhythm and blues number by Betty Everett, *You're No Good*, demonstrated Linda's capability as a torchy blues singer, with her wailing, expressive beratement. The song was backed by Clydie King and Shirley Matthews and Linda lets out with a kind of powerful yet mournful wail of all the hurt that's expressed in the song—the ache of a million women bruised and knocked about by the captivating ne'er do wells they're attracted to.

Another resonating track on the album was *Faithless Love*, by J. D. Souther. It's a strong, powerful ballad which was well suited to Linda's talents and featured Herb Pederson on the banjo in a tangy accompaniment against Linda's lead vocal.

The title song, written by Anna McGarrigle, is a folk hymn which was impressive in its eloquence and tastefulness, almost an elegant tone poem with its simplicity and its soulfulness. There were no tacky lyrics, no catchy, cutesie phrases, just from the heart vocals that Linda expresses so

well in song. Perhaps this song more than anything else on the album projected what was to become Linda Ronstadt's personality as a performer—her aching heart suffering from lost and gone wrong love, but she's strong enough to try again and go through it all, the toughness to cope with the dilemma of needing love but not wanting to be knocked about. And the knowledge that it was love more than any other emotion which would upset her and tear apart her insides. It was this vulnerable yet tough personality flavor which became the stamp of Linda Ronstadt.

Heart Like A Wheel unified all the diverse musical influences of Linda's singing. She assembled country and rock and blues and folk with this album, and integrated her vocal style. A good indication of this achievement is the fact that Heart fared well not only on the pop charts but also did well on the country album charts.

Linda began to enjoy what success felt like with *Heart Like A Wheel*, and it was very pleasant for her.

As she told a New York Times interviewer early in 1975, "Well, I'm obviously pleased. And finally I'll make some money. But the day Peter Asher called to say the album was doing really well, I was sick in bed with the flu—the fever was so bad I saw lizards on the walls—and there was dirty laundry everywhere. And even with a hit record, no angels appeared and said, 'You'll always be healthy and you'll never have any dirty laundry again.' "

Heart Like A Wheel not only established Linda Ronstadt as a powerful and important rock star, but it also marked the development of the personality that is so alluring to rock audiences today, the combustible combination of sensuality in her stance and attitude and the little girl innocence of her dress in boy-scout uniforms and knee socks, leaping around on stage with no shoes on. She started performing for audiences in cub scout uniforms, as she did recently, and cultivated a kind of girlish sexiness by doing so. Linda says she feels uncomfortable performing in a dress. She explains that she wore shorts one night almost by accident. The night before she had worn a dress that made her feel uncomfortable and stilted and stupid, and by mistake her wardrobe mistress brought the same dress the next night for a performance. She knew she couldn't wear that dress again and go through the agonizing discomfort of that so she decided to wear shorts.

"I sing better according to what I wear. First of all, all these summer gigs are real hot because they're in outdoor pavilions. It's real muggy and hot and you can't wear anything that's going to be hot to start with. And there's something about sports clothes that lend themselves to movement, to feeling a little bit freer with your body. They also look real good. ... Sometimes I like dresses, but they're difficult and awkward and all. It's sort of like when you would go to the prom and do the bob in your formal. ... You would feel stupid."

But as Linda was accentuating the come-hither personal style that would woo audiences, she was not allowing her musical development to rest idly by. The critics who lauded *Heart Like A Wheel* as nothing less than a triumph and the full blossoming of Linda's talents were even more stunned by the depth of achievement and musical sensibility revealed in her next album, *Prisoner in Disguise*. Where *Heart Like A Wheel* could be described as a collection of stunning and congenial records, *Prisoner in Disguise* showed Linda as a daring experimenter, willing to take vocal chances that showed her tremendous versatility.

The album began with a haunting song by Neil Young called *Love Is Like A Rose*, which although not varying much from the traditional Ronstadt

mode, was still a marvelous showcase for her talents and the heartache quality she projects so well. It's a rhythmic song with Gospel shading and warns of the painful tears that love can bring to the heart. And the song, as is characteristic of Ronstadt's music under Asher's guidance, was expertly produced and well harmonized. Then *Heat Wave*, originally sung by the black group Martha and the Vandellas, was a gusty and glimmery tune that captured her knack for conveying a song's movement and stirring beat. It's a brash, zesty number that again captures the energy of Linda's mobile voice.

But as good as she was on the soul songs, the best cuts from *Prisoner* are the ones which display the full range and thoughtfulness that Linda can carry forth in her music. Her ability to graft other idioms onto a song in another tradition is demonstrated with Smokey Robinson's *Tracks of My Tears*, which is not just another version in the Motown vein. Linda's unique vocalizing brings this song a tangy country flavor that gives it an original perspective, a new slant on a golden oldie which is what she likes to do. It's a surprising look at an old standard, which shows how Linda can gain new interpretations out of old music.

She does a superb job with James Taylor's version of *Hey Mister that's Me Up on the Jukebox*, which spells out how she's got spunk even while singing sad, bottomed out, bluesy songs. It fits Linda's voice wonderfully.

She also essays the Dolly Parton tune, *I Will Always Love You*. The song is one of Dolly's best and its high range was well-suited for Parton's silvery vibrato. But Linda again manifests her incredible range and is able to wring many shades of meaning out of that one line. Near the finale, she repeats the title a few times and with each version gives a different delivery. The effect is haunting.

Linda's always been interested in the various types of ethnic music and so on this album she delved into the Jamaican cult song of reggae. The song is Jimmy Cliff's *Many Rivers to Cross*. The interpretation has usually been one of rousing Gospel spirit but Linda gives it her own stamp, turning it into another of her soulful lamentations where the lyrics emerge much more powerfully than even before. It's a powerful number and again, another way in which Linda gives a different shading to a song that has been done in a traditional manner.

The title song is written by one of Linda's old friends and a former producer of her records, John David Souther. The song again creates the main themes of the album, the entanglements and complexities of romance and the cool and clever games people play to deal with it.

Linda again goes into a mournful cry about love with *You Tell Me That*

I'm Falling Down by Carole Holland and Anna McGarrigle who wrote the haunting *Heart Like A Wheel*. The song is about ridicule and heartbreak, common threads in the Ronstadt material, and is spun out with the most complete faith as if the words had been wrung out of Linda's hurting heart. This is one of those songs that Linda obviously knows from first hand experience what the words mean.

More in the rock mode is *Roll Um Easy* by Lowell George with a hefty beat and a slide guitar background. Linda then teams up with Emmylou Harris from some haunting vocalizing on *The Sweetest Gift*, a traditional country song with affectionate poignancy.

The band which backed Linda on *Prisoner in Disguise* was an outstanding one, led by a talented musician named Andrew Gold. They provided the sense of integration that was lacking on some of her previous albums where the music seemed to stray off in many directions. There was also a capable new pianist named Brock Walsh. As Linda explained the situation, "I always have a masculine figure interpret for me—I try to work through him. If you're going to be a musician, you have to compete with the boys."

Prisoner in Disguise could be considered even more of a triumph than *Heart Like A Wheel* because Linda was experimenting with so many new types of material. She was tackling a fresher, more original approach.

Ronstadt's next album was *Hasten Down the Wind*. It received mixed reviews and Linda herself acknowledged that it was a very "down" album. "I was very depressed then," she admits. The criticisms were the usual of her work—spotty material with uneven quality and a kind of automatic approach to some of the numbers.

But *Hasten Down the Wind* did represent a change from her other albums. The songs on *Hasten* were quite different. For instance, there were no renditions of black hits or country standards. This meant that much of the buoyancy was gone, with a more leaden, heavy quality in the music. It's beautiful and soulful singing but there is almost a deadening sense of depression about the entire album, rife as it is with heartbreak and sadness and the kind of deep love laments that she is famous for.

Even her songwriters are different. There are no tunes from her old reliable composers, John David Souther and James Taylor. Instead, she tries works by artists she has never recorded before, such as Warren Zevon, Tracy Nelson and Karla Bonoff. And as a special bonanza for Ronstadt fans, there are two songs which she worked on herself. Not surprisingly, both are weighty with emotion and evoke the same kind of teary poignancy like the other cuts on the album. *Try Me Again* is a

personal confession; the Spanish-styled *Lo Sienta Mi Vida* is written with Kenny Edwards and her father.

She sings the old hit by Willie Nelson called *Crazy*, which was originally recorded by Patsy Cline, a top country singer. The song is not a predictable one for Linda; its nuances are much too subtle for her large and powerful voice but she brings to the jazz-tinged love ballad a kind of sultry vampishness and torchiness that is almost violent in its wrenching quality.

Picking up again from Buddy Holly and his throbbing rock tunes, she gives a rendition of *That'll Be The Day*, which was to become a big single hit for her. The rousing quality of the song is tempered by the kind of plaintive way she delivers it. There's a kind of bitter quality, however, that pervades this song, as there is with the Karla Bonoff tune, *Someone to Lay Down Beside Me*. With these kinds of songs, Ronstadt builds from a strong beginning to a powerful, rocking kind of climax.

More in the country vein is *The Tattler*, by Ry Cooder. It offers some advice to the lovelorn, as only Linda can effectively deliver. Then there's *Give One Heart*, by John and Johanna Hall which also tenders a bit of homespun counseling from the sadder but wiser gal and *Down So Low*, by Tracy Nelson. *Down So Low* is almost anguishing in its powerful portrayal of a woman so defeated by a lost love.

The effect of the album is devastating—it's so forceful in its power that it's hard to come away from it unaffected. And the feeling is even two-pronged. On the one hand there's the creative elation one feels from Linda's dazzling vocal efforts, almost like a mesmerizing blues singer. On the other, the total effect of the songs is very depressing. There is a feeling of great grief in the album. Nevertheless, some rock critics regard it as Linda's best because it effectively captures all the nuances of her songs and offers material which she is obviously close to.

Simple Dreams, Linda's next album, was far brighter and more optimistic in tone. It looked like Linda had pulled herself out of the depression rut. Obviously in a more upbeat frame of mind, Linda joked after the album was released that listeners would either think that she was "real sick" or had a great sense of humor. "I was definitely laughing a lot on this album," she admitted with a sunny smile.

Linda had executed some major musical changes with the release of *Simple Dreams*. Andrew Gold, the lead musician who had guided her band since her first blockbusting album *Heart Like A Wheel* in 1974, had left the Ronstadt entourage to go out on his own. He had played a key role in the arrangements and the presentations of what Linda sang.

But as his style matured and became more individualistic, it was incongruous with the band's unity. And Andrew Gold wanted to make his kind of music, not the kind of music that was simply a backdrop to that of Linda's. He was replaced by Waddy Wachtel and things became a lote more aggressive, according to Linda. It was Kenny Edwards who was responsible for bringing Waddy and Linda together.

Simple Dreams offers a complex assortment of songs, with some folk tunes, some vintage oldies newfangled by Linda, and a Rolling Stone number called *Tumbling Dice.*

One of the most moving numbers is one called *Blue Bayou,* crafted by that famous country composer, Roy Orbison. Ronstadt delivers a haunting refrain of a lost and forgotten paradise, etched forever in memory. The song is filled with such yearning and longing that it reaches all the depths of emotionality that Linda, at her finest, is capable of.

Simple Dreams, Linda claims, is definitely an autobiographical album. It begins with the old and popular Buddy Holly song, *It's So Easy,* which again recounts the familiar Ronstadt theme of falling in love and getting bruised. The song talks about vulnerability and about the risk of involvement and infatuation, both of which have gotten Linda into trouble in her personal life time and again. She has said that the songs on the first side the album definitely portray her story.

"When you're a teenager or in your early 20's, romance is the whole thing," she says. "I thought so anyway, and so did most of my friends. We sat around the Troubadour bar every night waiting to meet just the right guy.

"If you weren't in love, you pretended you were. Then all the problems came ... the fights, the breakups. Love didn't turn out to be so easy after all. There were always scars."

But Linda often covered up the scars with humor. Two songs that she does by Warren Zevon—*Poor, Poor Pitiful Me* and *Carmelita* display the kind of kinky humor that Zevon is famous for. They both show that Linda is approaching her life with some perspective.

Linda remembers her first meeting with the offbeat Zevon. Despite how impressed she was by his previous reputation on his debut album produced by Jackson Browne—she thought, she confesses kiddingly, that he looked like a psychopath. He came backstage, along with a crowd of other well-wishers and congratulators, after a Ronstadt concert. She recalls that he stood there, kind of speechless, scratching his head absent-mindedly, with no words coming out of his mouth, just opening and closing it in embarrassment.

But despite this inauspicious beginning, Linda and Zevon became good friends and she discovered what a shy and sensitive person he was—totally unlike that erroneous first impression.

Linda says that *Poor, Poor Pitiful Me* and *Carmelita* were two songs that she was always interested in recording but was hesitant to do them because the lyrics were so strong. But, as her confidence swelled and grew, she felt capable of doing the Zevon numbers.

Carmelita, which follows *It's So Easy* on the record album is a natural follow-up to the Buddy Holly song. Where one celebrates the pitfalls of being in love, the second recounts the aftermath of the breakup, when you feel depressed and blue and more careful about falling in love again. Specifically, the song is about a strung-out heroin addict who fantasizes about a Tijuana love. Linda speaks of the broken romances in your past which make you put up defenses to love in the future.

The next song, *Sorrow Lives Here*, Linda believes is about the search for companionship when you're alone. The song, Linda feels, is about facades and false appearances, which happen to a person who's been hurt in love—the old tension between vulnerability and invincibility. Interestingly, the next song is perhaps a more definitive statement of where Linda's heart lies. It is the country traditional *I Never Will Marry*, by Dolly Parton and Dolly joins Linda for the choruses. The result is one of the most moving songs Linda has ever recorded. The lyrics are aptly suited to Linda's steadfast claims to remaining single and her vows to stay away from the marital state.

But *I Never Will Marry* is not just a vow for the future. It is also an expression of how difficult it is for Linda to marry and maintain her career. Not being married allows her the freedom to let a lot of different people into her life—yet it also gives her the pain which can be felt by multiple relationships.

But lest her listeners think that Linda is into a downtrodden lament about her romantic vicissitudes, she pulls a fast one with the spunky, self-poking fun tune by Zevon, *Poor, Poor Pitiful Me*. The tune is almost a parody of what has been called Linda's dark self-pity. In its black humored cry of despair, it is almost like a melodic counterpart to Dorothy Parker's famous poem about the disadvantages of various methods of suicide. One refrain tells how Linda, or the singer, contemplates laying her head on the railroad tracks, but alas, the train isn't running anymore.

One of the gayest moments on the album is the lusty and raunchy *Tumbling Dice* which Linda learned from Mick Jagger during her brief but well-publicized relationship with him. Linda, realizing that despite her

country talents and her exquisitely plaintive laments, she also had her rock ability to draw on, began taking an avid interest in the music of the Stones. *Tumbling Dice* became a favorite encore, with Linda delivering it with rousing fervor, as gustily as the jumping and leaping Stones could do under the nimble prancing of Jagger.

How did Linda become interested in a song which is not her usual fare? She explains that her band would play *Tumbling Dice* during sound check at concerts. When Mick Jagger came backstage after a concert, he advised her to do more rock sounds instead of ballads, so Linda thought over what he said and asked him to write down the words for *Tumbling Dice*. She learned them and started including the song in her concerts, then released it as one of the highlights in her 1977 album, *Simple Dreams*.

Tumbling Dice is on the second side of the album, which has a compelling blend of country, bluegrass, rock and roll, showing that Linda can excell at many musical modes. After rocking and rolling her way through *Tumbling Dice*, she continues with the countrified *Blue Bayou* and then concludes with *Old Paint*, a zippy cowgirl song that she certainly delights in.

Two other cuts on the album include *Maybe I'm Right*, the first song recorded by her guitar player, Waddy Wachtel, and the title song, *Simple Man, Simple Dream*, by her favorite song craftsman, J. D. Souther. Both of these are poignant ballads delivered in the usually excellent heartwringing Ronstadt manner.

"I think *Simple Dreams* is a great statement about California music," Linda says. The critics considered the album a great statement about the magnificent quality of Ronstadt's talent.

Glowed the New York Post, "This album casts its spell like the windows at Tiffany's with elegant elements carefully arranged to show off some bewitching gem. The jewel is Ronstadt's unmistakeable soprano voice."

And the New York Times rhapsodized about its "more basic arrangements and a growing maturity and strength in her music and her persona." *Simple Dreams* marked a quantum leap for Linda musically.

Linda's newest entry in the pop-rock album sweepstakes is *Living in the U.S.A.* The cover of it features another coy picture of Linda, ever the photographer's mugger. She's got some shorts on and those striped kneesocks she's always performing in now. Plus a short satin battle jacket and she's striding atop her favorite new shoes—roller skates. She's also sporting a shorter, hipper, curlier hairdo, and the album projects the kind of upbeat, comfortable image that is portrayed on the cover.

Living in the U.S.A. features Linda's most varied song selections to date.

There are numbers by Romberg—*When I Grow too Old to Dream*—songs by the two Elvises—Presley and Costello—and also tunes by Oscar Hammerstein, Chuck Berry and Smokey Robinson. Linda seems to have dared even more vocally with this album—it's another conquest for her.

She hits the rock beat hard with *Back in the U.S.A.*, the Chuck Berry classic, then segues into a tenderly romantic 1934 standard—the haunting *When I Grow too Old to Dream*, by Romberg and Hammerstein, a true lullaby. She switches tone then with the soul hit *Just One Look* and then demonstrates further versatility and range with songs by Elvis, Elvis Costello, Warren Zevon and Eric Kaz.

There's a haunting number called *All That You Dream* by Little Feat and then Zevon's *Mohammed's Radio* and Kaz' *Blowing Away*.

But perhaps one of the most hearttugging numbers is the Elvis classic *Love Me Tender*.

How Linda came about recording the song *Back in the U.S.A.* is indicative of her current good moods. She recalls driving around with Eagles singer Glenn Frey, reminiscing about the way back when times when they used to hang out at the Troubadour and sigh about when they'd ever get a record deal. They were flat broke and miserable and down and out then. Recalling what had transpired in the meantime, how Linda was now sitting in the car with both of them rich and successful, she started pledging her patriotism. She also realized that she felt happier than she'd felt in years. Then *Back in the U.S.A.* came on the radio and Linda, very optimistic and content and happy with herself at that point, said that she'd like to record that bouncy tune. And so she did.

The song also expresses what Linda feels is a better attitude toward the U.S.A. It indicates a rise in patriotism and more positive feelings about America, a swing-back from the malcontent and uprising-filled malaise of the 1960's. People are, according to Linda, realizing just how good the U.S.A. has become and Chuck Berry's lines which talk about drive-ins, hamburgers, jukeboxes, all celebrate the joys of American living and pop culture.

The song *Mohammed's Radio* by Zevon speaks to Linda in a very different way. She considers the song very well-written and sings it quite seriously and controlledly. The power of the radio as expressed in the song holds the same kind of mesmerizing, calming quality for Linda. "It's omnipresent, and it's powerful and almost godlike," she explains, quietly. And she feels the problems of grinding your way through life which can be hard and mean and petty, can actually be resolved by simply listening to the radio. Linda gets off on the music, it's her escape

and her solace. She talks about waiting for something wonderful to happen in the music, listening to songs and waiting for that epiphany-like moment when all the rest that plagues and bothers her just seems to float away.

Perhaps more than any other pop artist, listening to the albums of Linda Ronstadt is like watching her life develop, observing the inner changes that have been wrought as she's evolved into a more confident stage and self-assured and in-control singer. More than anything else, the album tells Linda's story as she's transformed herself over the years. Her current album is more than anything else a celebration of her vocal talents and her musical sounds—and that's probably summed up in the first word of the title—*Living*. That's what Linda is finally learning to do— "live" and enjoy.

6

Linda Ronstadt once said, "The only thing I ever try to state is just the day-to-day struggle of being a human being, in this day and age."

If nothing else, Linda is a very human personality; her super-stardom has not made her any less approachable. Her struggles, her pain, her bitterness, her happiness, her alternating moods of joviality with sadness, have all been chronicled in her music, even represented in her stance before an audience. When Linda is unhappy and feeling insecure, she slinks back from her fans and remains controlled and repressed in her singing style. When she's feeling exuberant and upbeat, she bounces up and down, throws herself into her songs, teases and laughs and giggles.

She's no glossy, highly slicked-up and plasticized performer like Diana Ross or Barbra Streisand, projecting a kind of pop, glistening image that leaves the person underneath pretty much a mystery. You know how Linda feels, what she thinks, where her head is at.

At an interview, she's candid and brutally honest about her difficulties

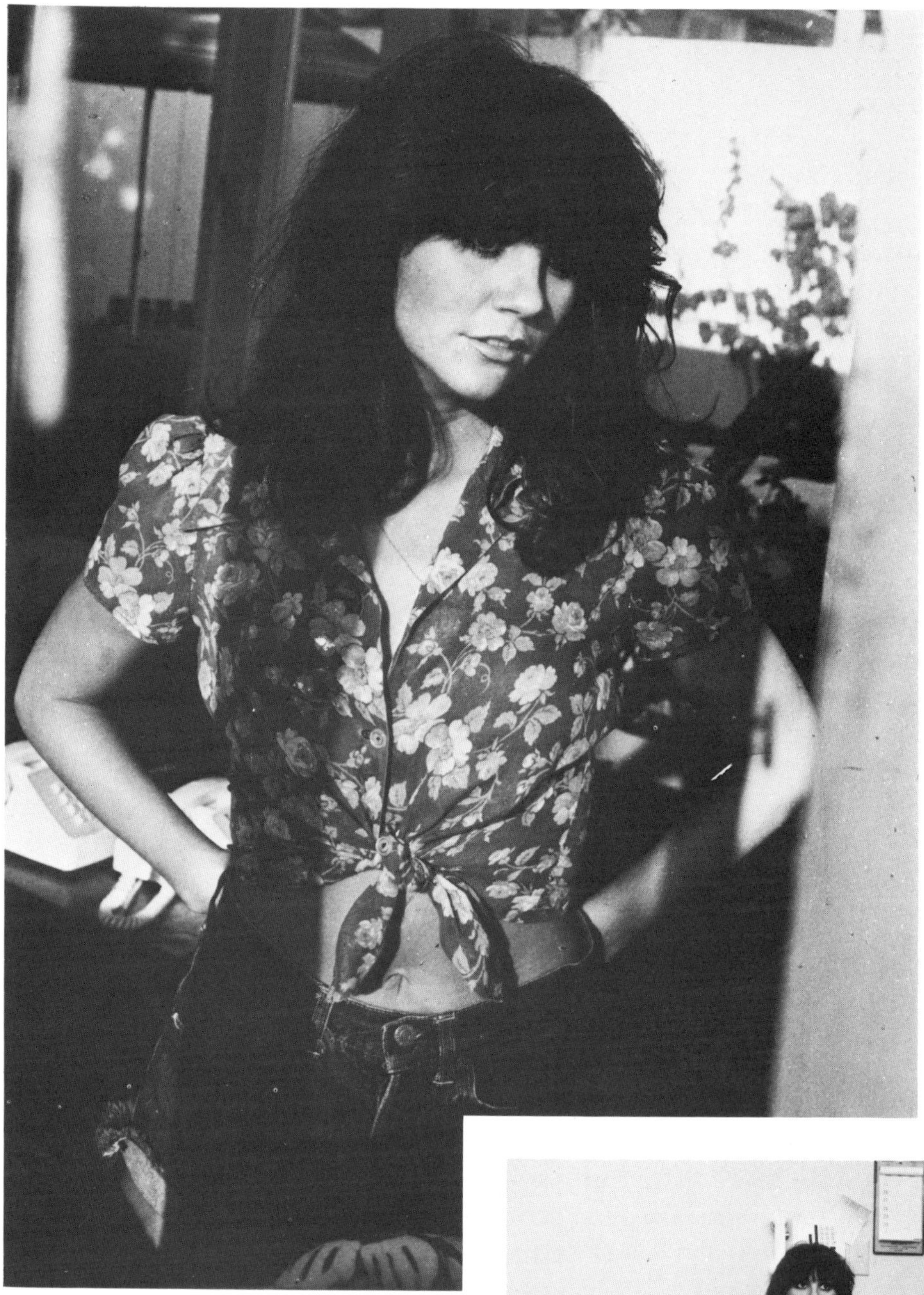

Taking a break at home.

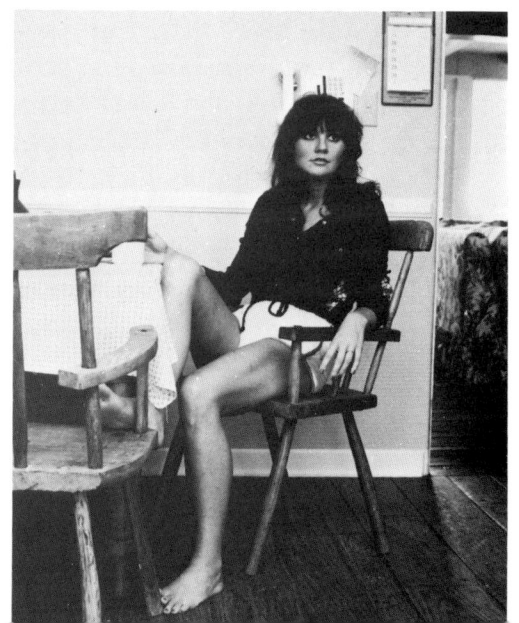

with her music and her love life. Sometimes this honesty, unusual in a public performer, can be damaging. Linda refuses to hide behind a web of confusing, pseudo-intellectual quotes. And the media love to capitalize on her frankly revealed pain.

As she laments, "You tell them that you have felt suicidal—who hasn't?—that you had the idea of wading into the ocean in North Carolina and swimming to New York. Then that comes out in a magazine and it becomes a permanent fact about you, when really it's just momentary."

But then she delves into the dangerous waters of self-confession again when she admits that "Anybody can hurt my feelings; it's not very hard to do. But they don't get a second chance." There's a tension between the tough and tender in this rock and roll queen. At the same time that Linda talks about her vulnerability, it's obvious that she can handle herself quite well in most situations.

The confessions, despite whatever public embarrassment she has experienced, keep coming. Linda's oft-expressed preference for Oreo cookies is one of the more harmless disclosures—they now arrive by the boxful at her hotel suite when she checks into town. Some performers are greeted with bouquets of roses; Linda's happier with the cookies that are sent up by messenger.

But it's all part of the two sides of Linda—one excited, vibrant, fun-loving, capricious and playful, the other depressed, anxious, somewhat tortured, afraid. Whichever side crops up, gets exposed; Linda doesn't masquerade.

Consider these two very different looks at Linda Ronstadt. During an interview with a correspondent with Time magazine, Linda prances around the room, obviously excited and happy, skips, does some deep knee bends, reminisces with giggly punctuation about her youth in Tucson, exclaims over her new Frye boots, calls for room service for orders as small as a stick of gum or a Tab—and always tips generously. When she's up, she's really up.

But when the nerves take over and she becomes frightened and unsure of herself, this bouncy, perky image of Linda recedes and a darker side emerges.

She's rehearsing for a concert and things are not going well. She's clearly nervous and upset—you can tell by the way her speech trails off into nervous giggles and queasy little snickers. She keeps tugging fretfully at her jeans, probably worrying that she looks fat, or that she looks bad. Her chatter between songs is awkward, slow. She appears to be standing

around, waiting for the band to end its numbers, or else waiting for the band to start the introduction so she can start singing. At one point she gets really frustrated and hurls a tambourine petulantly across the stage. She's twitchy and unsure of herself, and like anything else with Linda, it definitely shows.

She's uncomfortable too when the camera gets too close, when the fans start to pry, when the limelight focuses too relentlessly on Linda Ronstadt the singer. The mantle of superstardom is not one she wears easily. Once during a television appearance, Linda arrived on set with her face conspicuously broken out, a rather large pimple on her left cheek. After the make-up man tried different ways to cover it up, he finally wound up sticking a piece of glitter on it. When Linda saw the taping, she wailed in typical self-critical fashion, "Boy, I don't do anything right, do I? Now I got a chrome zit."

Perhaps it is this shaky self-esteem that makes Linda so unself-conscious and unassuming about her star status. She's appealingly unpretentious, without a speck of the arrogance that performers of less than her stature have. She's the type to call a restaurant and ask about their dress code, without ever identifying herself as Linda Ronstadt. It wouldn't occur to her to do that.

Linda really doesn't think of herself as a star. What she reaps pleasure from is being a good singer and getting the kudos she wants from peers in her own field. The other bonuses, the famous labels and the attention, "just make me more nervous," she says. "You know, 'cause it's something to kind of live up to."

Perhaps because she is genuinely down-to-earth, Linda lacks the ruthless competitiveness and jealousies harbored by other women in the cutthroat world of rock music. She's enthusiastic and even helpful about other female singers.

As she told The Boston Phoenix, "Competition if for race horses, not for art. I had to face all that when Emmylou Harris came on the scene. Everyone was telling me for two years that there was this girl who was doing everything that I was doing, and they were raving about her. I felt threatened by it, I was afraid: I was afraid to meet her. I thought, 'Oh no, what if she's better than I am?' and I met her and she was. I feel that she is the best country-rock person. I'm moving in more of a pop direction anyway. And I was stunned because I had been doing this for a long time and I knew exactly how her talents compared to mine. And I also loved her immediately when I met her, because she's honest and she's nice. There was no way I couldn't like her."

Linda finds it unsettling to be in the constant face of attention with her face so readily recognizable. She complains that she doesn't like it when she's in a restaurant eating dinner and someone comes up and asks for her autograph. "It's a distraction and it's an annoyance and they don't realize it's rude." And the lack of privacy has become more of a burden than ever in the last few years, since she achieved more celebrity than ever. She can recount horror stories about the swarming of mobs around her—she was almost "jumped on" when she and some friends went to a beach club on the Fourth of July and on St. Patrick's Day in New York, she found herself being chased—and she emphasizes the word "chased" with a grimace—down the streets. The lack of privacy and the spectacle of her life that show business has triggered tends to make Linda feel on the defensive. It makes her uneasy sometimes when she's not performing, just being Linda the person, shopping, walking, eating, driving. She doesn't like to be a public personality.

She says with a frown, "What it does is it makes people look like enemies all the time, 'cause you never know what someone's going to do."

Plainly, she doesn't enjoy the star trappings. Linda would rather just get up and sing and then go home. She doesn't care for the fanfare. "I don't think of myself as a star," she insists, "I just wanted to become a singer. The star part is just something they made up in Hollywood in 1930."

But stardom means success, and in terms of pop appeal and in terms of commercial value of records and concerts appearances, Linda is certainly successful. What does all this success mean to her? It's not the money nor the acclaim nor the masses of admirers that matter. It is simply a question of doing things better professionally because now she has the financial wherewithal and the clout.

"I used to think that success would solve all your problems," she says with a sigh. "Success does mean you get to work with the best musicians, have the best sound equipment and have the best people handling your tours. That's a big help. But it doesn't get rid of your personal problems."

For in spite of all the admiration and respect and phenomenal success in monetary terms, Linda's found that life can be just as troublesome—perhaps even more so because when you're a superstar of Linda's magnitude, it can be lonely. Things are even tougher when you're a girl singer, although through the years it's gotten easier for women to handle success in the tough waters of the rock music world. It's a time for breaking through for women singers and Linda's been in the vanguard of

that movement. And she's managed to retain her femininity at the same time, unlike the late rock star Janis Joplin, who assumed a gravelly personality to match her gravelly voice to make it big and to do so became one of the boys.

But then American tastes in music have changed and the sweeter sound is the female voice which has triumphed in the macho word of rock. It used to be, as Linda says, female singers "lived under the shadow of Tina Turner, feeling we had to do hot blues licks—or be considered a little butch."

"That's the way the business was in those days," she observes. But along came girl singers—the emphasis should be on the word girl—like Stevie Nicks and Christie McVie of Fleetwood Mac and Linda mentions the Wilson sisters of Heart. That's what made the femininity concept in rock important.

But Linda cites another person as being crucial in helping her combine femininity with success in the music world and that's Dolly Parton. Linda fairly idolizes Dolly, not only for her talent and her composing gifts, but also for her personal charm and fortitude of spirit. They were each admirers of the other from a distance, never meeting in person until Emmylou Harris brought the two together.

Linda is extravagantly rhapsodic when she talks about Dolly. "I've never met anybody so free of neurosis as that person," she says. "I was devastated by her honesty and her charm and sweetness. I'm sort of this Northern thinker and she's just kind of a Southern magnolia blossom that floats on the breeze."

It was Dolly, Linda claims, who taught her how to be aggressive and assertive with a dulcet touch. "Dolly taught me that you don't have to sacrifice your femininity to have equal status in this male-oriented business. The only thing that gives you equal status is your musicianship—period!"

Yet for all her proudly proclaimed independence and self-directedness, Linda is not a flamboyant Women's Lib flag bearer. In fact, she even says things that would make a diehard Women Libber's bristle. Like her belief that women are naturally more monogamous than men.

But she's more open to making women friends now and that's part of her increasing awareness of her womanhood. Linda's quite close with other female singers like Maria Muldaur, Karla Bonoff, Joni Mitchell and Bonnie Raitt, besides Emmylou and Dolly. And one of her fondest wishes is someday to start an informal all-woman group that would record and tour all over the country.

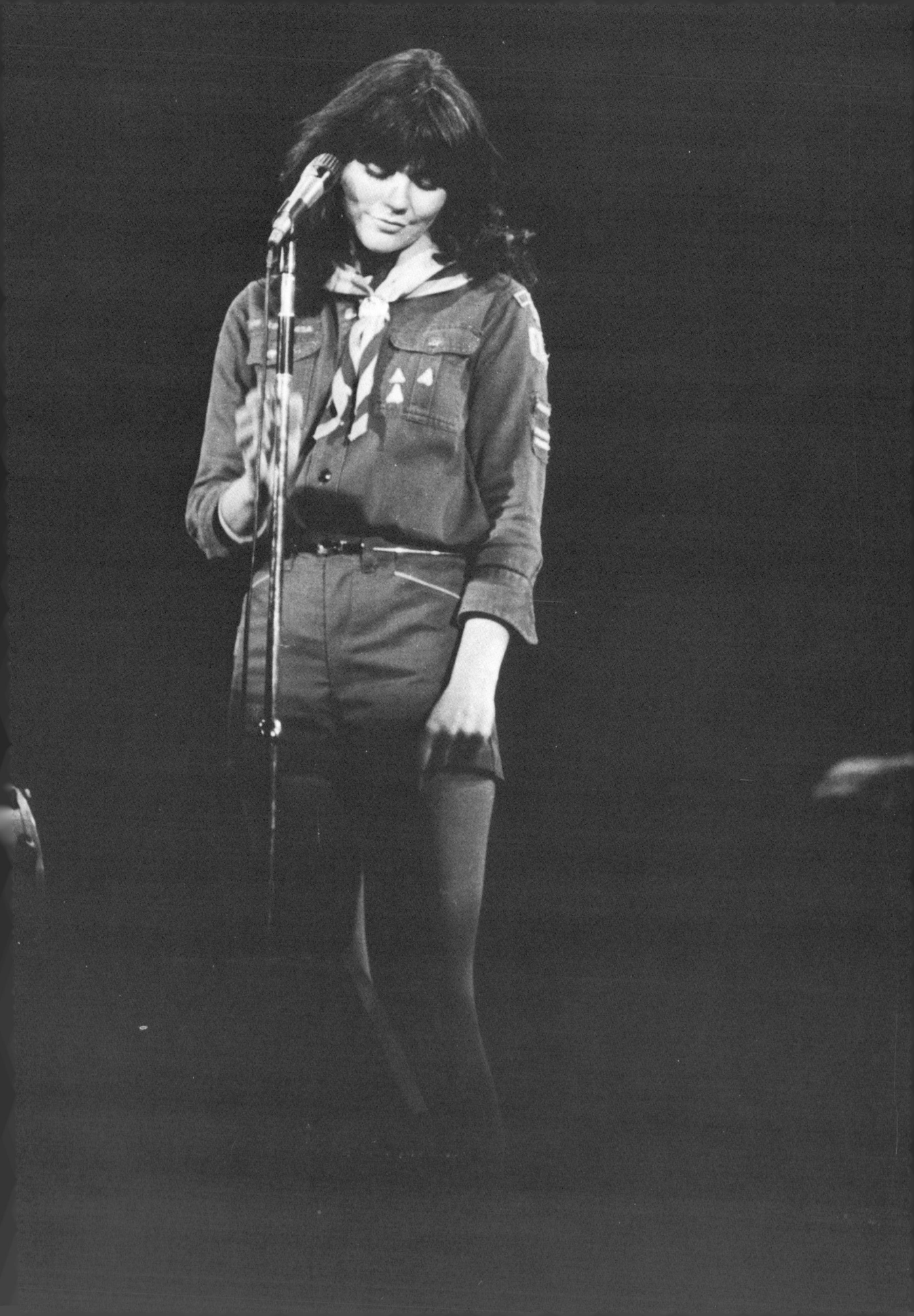

Since she is a woman singer and a popular one who makes an impressive spokeswoman, Linda is often queried on her feelings about the woman's movement.

"Sometimes people ask me why I'm not a feminist and that's really crazy. You see obviously I am, because I'm an independent woman; I have been since I was 18. I earn my own living. I'm dependent on no man, I'm a free agent."

One of the things that really riled her feminist beliefs was when Tammy Wynette made the record about standing by your man, urging that a woman's place be in the home. Because, Linda says, it wasn't quite fair for Tammy to evaluate a situation that way, since she has a career and wasn't frustrated or repressed in a professional sense, like so many house-bound wives are. It's the other kind of woman, the one who stays home and simply cooks and sews and tends the family quarters, that suffers.

For her part, Linda is expansive about how the woman's movement has helped her own life. As she revealed to Katharine Orloff in Rock 'n Roll Woman, "It has helped an awful lot. It has helped me realize where a lot of frustrations come from. Before, I was just sort of bogged down by them and couldn't quite figure out what I was supposed to be. Here I was a chick who traveled around and had an enormous amount of independence. I didn't relate to other men like other women did, and men didn't relate to me like they did to other women. Being more aware of things has helped me deal with it. I think the woman's movement is important. I think it's vital. I think it's important to men, too. ... I think it should reduce the tension between the sexes."

But it's not the subject of sexism but instead sexuality that so often occurs when Linda's name is brought up. With her torchy style of singing and especially those recently sported performing costumes of hot pants and high heels, Linda exudes sexiness. She is not what anyone could call classically beautiful, but she practices the fine art of being sexy to an expert degree. Her skin is plagued from time to time with acne—it breaks out when she's going through her bouts of nerves and nervousness, and her figure, certainly, although cutely appealing, is hardly reminiscent of Mae West. Her hair is flecked with gray. But there's a limpid and ultimately winsome charm in those wide brown eyes and a fetching sensuality that curls around her pouty lips. Linda knows and has said many times that she's far from being in the same category with Jean Harlow, of that exquisite make of face and body. But her philosophy is that attractiveness comes from a feeling about yourself.

"I don't think those things are essential to being attractive. Sometimes

Linda is a keen jogger and works out early morning on the beach beside her home.

they're more of a handicap than a help. I think vitality is what is attractive to people."

Her beauty creed has certainly worked well. So well that the people from the infamous girlie magazine called Hustler offered her the princely sum of one million dollars to pose in the nude for a centerfold. It wasn't surprising that rumors started sprouting that Linda was seriously contemplating the offer. Of course, she wasn't, but it seemed likely that she could have done so. After all, it would have been in the sensual Linda mode.

Besides her ardent feminist beliefs, another thing that may have stood in the way of Linda's posing for Hustler is an abiding and probably neurotic concern about her weight. She stands just 5-feet two-inches and because she's so petite, she constantly frets about her weight. She's always worrying about it—jabbing at her thighs, pulling at her stomach, poinding her hips. At her best, she slims down to some 107 to 110 pounds, but then her weight can balloon up again when she's on the road and nervous or bored.

"Food is my real addiction," she sighs regretfully. That's where her fondness for Oreos can become troublesome. When she's put on what she feels is too much weight, she spends some time at a fat farm usually a place called Ashram, which is really a small health spa in California.

As with many other subjects, Linda is thoughtful and articulate even on so mundane a matter as food. She grouses that the reason she has troubles with diet today is because she, as a child, was raised to clean off her plate. She also believes that food is a handy "boredom appeaser," handy to squelch the pangs of loneliness that occur when she's not working or those draughts of inactivity on the road. She tries to dress to appear thinner, and when she sports a pair of blue jeans and a blouse tied off at the waist, she claims it's not to make her look sexy, but thin.

Her tastes in food aren't always the healthiest which can contribute to her weight dilemma. Sometimes she'll order a big hunk of steak and other times, she'll order a range of junk food. Despite these erratic eating patterns, Linda says that she does try, in sporadic bursts, to be healthier. That's when she starts pouring the thick brewer's yeast into her orange juice.

To combat the eating binges and to feel better, Linda jogs—usually on the beach at her Malibu home and when she's on tour, she has one of those indoor devices so she can run inside. She also does exercises with weights—which she keeps in her room, at the studio, and even on the truck during tours.

Linda is one of those jogging fanatics, another of the breed who feels that the sport is definitely a cure-all. She herself finds it is the only effective cure for the crippling periods of depression that plague her. Depression is a real and troublesome problem for Linda—she thinks that it basically affects women more than men and that it is a troublesome problem for her. "I'm so afraid of it now that it stops me completely cold," she says. "If I get depressed, I just go to bed for a week."

But thankfully those dark and gloomy periods of depression and despair don't come as frequently as they used to. Part of the reason is that during a real down period in her life Linda entered psychotherapy with a psychiatrist who she thinks really helped her turn her life around—he made her see that she was worthy of her success, that there was no reason for Linda to go around apologizing for her popularity and the money she makes.

The money is phenomenal and it's made Linda a millionairess, but it's not something she's really into. For a long time she went through what she refers to as "the investment stage" of her career because she went out

LINDA RONSTADT

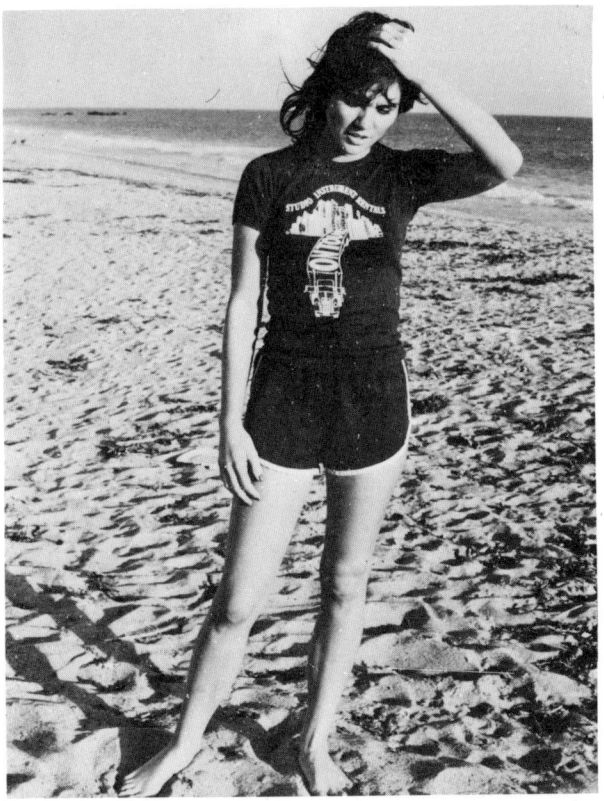

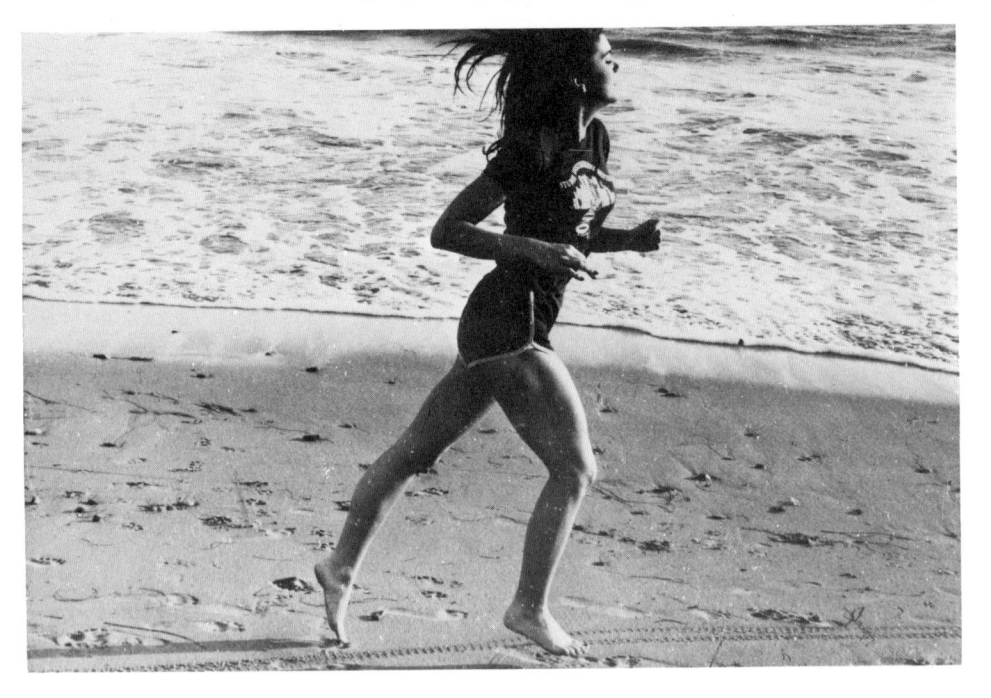

on tours and often wound up deeply in debt. One year alone she toted up more than $100,000 and still lost money after she paid her traveling and equipment costs and other things which drained her finances.

Her recording costs are high too because she likes to use the very best musicians and the best equipment to get the sounds the way she likes them. And, unlike other singers, she doesn't increase her income by reaping royalties from songs. So the tremendous costs which Linda accrues are merely defrayed by the records and the concerts and nothing else.

And Linda does live simply for someone of her celebrity caliber. She's not into a fancy, gilded lifestyle. For example, she doesn't buy designer clothes or go in for the kind of conspicuous consumption that other stars indulge in. Before one tour, Linda had a fancy, big-name designer create several expensive outfits for her to wear onstage. But she hardly wore them; they remained in the closet most of the time. Instead, she preferred to appear in more casual, less dressy numbers like hot pants and a cute Cub Scout outfit she discovered.

Her pleasures other than singing are modest ones. She doesn't participate in expensive hobbies or super-chic activities. She has a puppy named Jenny that she dotes on. She often invites friends over to tea, especially her women friends. What she likes best of all, though, in the way of entertainment, is to have people over for dinner. Linda protests that she's not very good at cooking but she does claim to bake excellent bread.

She glows when she speaks of these at-home evenings with the people she's fond of and feels comfortable with. "When there are people that are close and my little brother Mike and Marilyn and Lois, these people are all in the kitchen and we're sitting around and Nicky's always got her guitar and we're singing or something like that. I mean, to me that's heaven, that's my favorite thing to do."

Home for Linda used to be a modest beachhouse in Malibu, which in the pricey community of Hollywood, only cost some $325,000. It was probably her single extravagance. Made out of white clapboard, it is most comfortably and cosily furnished and reflects a serious domestic streak in Linda. She bought some good china and silverware to go with it, to serve those dinners for her friends. The china is also used at her famous tea parties, which are frequently attended by a neighborhood girl of about seven, with whom Linda gets along famously.

But now Linda's giving up the Malibu house. One of the reasons is her cherished sanctuary was violated when a magazine printed her address

and fans came up to her home in wild, frenetic hordes. Linda was furious that her privacy was violated like that.

But there's another reason for her exodus from the Malibu house. And that's that Linda feels that Los Angeles and its surrounding communities are no longer where the main music action is, like in the 60's. Linda has planned a move to New York City, a place which she believes is more in the hub of the music industry than before, and has a place which generates more energy in general. You might say that she's tired of that characteristic California laid-back lifestyle, and she wants a refreshing change of climate and atmosphere.

Of course one of the problems that emerges because of the move is that Linda will be far away from her family, with whom she is very close. They all lead very different, much more normal and usual lives than Linda, their superstar sister. Her sister Gretchen, is married and has children. Her brother Pete is a policeman, and younger brother Michael wants to become a singer but is still in the fledgling stages.

As Linda told Broadside, speaking about her ties with her family, "They haven't got time to go running around, doing that kind of

nonsense, but I sing with them every time I go home. In fact, I'm thinking very seriously of using them to sing with me. ... It's something I've always wanted to do, more than anything else, make a record with them. ... We sound good together; we've got a good blend, seeing as we're all from the same womb."

Part of that sameness has instilled a capacity in her for hard work and the kind of determination that made her a celebrity and respected early in her career. The desire to move to New York may also be a wish on Linda's part to rev up her system and get into a high-pressure milieu that will renew her music and her art. There have been bouts of idleness, but that has been more from anxiety and apprehension than indifference to work. It's the fear that can paralyze her, Linda claims.

"Laziness is a real tricky word. Laziness is really fear. I'm not afraid of hard work, even of drudgery. It's just that I was scared because I didn't know what to do. My taste developed faster than my craft, and my frustration tolerance was real low. I was terrified that if I actually sat down and tried to learn to play the guitar and work out my songs, that my phrasing wouldn't improve because I really just didn't have it to start with."

So she told New Times, to explain those periods when the moods prevent her from accomplishing much.

It's a whole new period in Linda's life, a much more open and experimental period than before. As she becomes more confident of her talent and ability—and with so many gold records, it's no wonder that the self-assurance is growing—she's more relaxed and willing to be let-down and honest with more people. Linda is enjoying a kind of camaraderie with people that she never appreciated to such a great extent before. She's much more involved with friends and women and the support system makes her feel terrific. That's why Linda goes out of her way to promote a new singer or to compliment someone she finds really worthy of acclaim in the music world. At times, in interviews, she'll spend much of the time talking about another woman singer instead of elaborating on her own talents.

As she says of her relationships with other women, "We have to depend on each other. In the old days we couldn't afford psychiatrists. Maria Muldaur, Bonnie Raitt, Wendy Waldman and I kept each other from having nervous breakdowns for years. And my attitude towards anyone who is new on the horizon is that if they're good, and it's honest, then it has to be helped; those people have to be brought in. My feeling about girls that are better than I am is that we need 'em because they'll

make the music better, and I can learn from them. There's always somebody who's better than you."

Actually, Linda has confessed that she doesn't even like the sound of her own voice that much. It's not false modesty, she claims, but rather a case that is typical of many singers—they just feel embarrassed and uncomfortable listening to their own voices on records or on tapes. Linda calls her voice "nasal and harsh and a little constricted." It's something that irritates her but she says she can't do anything about it. But then Linda has always been a harsh critic of herself.

Now Linda's becoming more assertive and that includes taking more credit and less criticism. As she records more and more albums, she finds that she's more in control of the entire project and she likes that. She used to prefer to have everything dictated to her and give up the responsibility. These days she wants to pick the musicians and select the music and the style of the arrangements—it's as much of her job as hitting the notes.

It's all part of the move from aloneness and a more solitary way of life to a peopled kind of existence. Because of her refusal to be tied and committed to a nuclear family-type existence, she struggles with feelings

of floating and disconnectedness that affect her a lot. But in recent times, she's been making an effort to get more people involved in her life and become closer to those who mean something to her, who treat her as Linda and not as Linda Ronstadt. Much to her chagrin, Linda confesses that some close friends started treating her like a star, but in the end they didn't last at all.

It's still hard for people to get close to Linda and for her to get close to people, but it's getting better. The problem is that because she's a star, some people seek her out because they want something and she's well aware of that. Often it's the most aggressive that can get to her, while the more sincere, and honest kind of friends find it difficult to get through. Linda says that she has to assume a somewhat "standoffish" aspect because otherwise the users would devour her. As she explained her position to Rolling Stone, "You have to sort of erect a fence and say, 'Okay, scale this.' It's like living on top of a glass mountain."

But then Linda's position has always been a precarious one. She's never played it easy and doesn't plan to go the safe route now. She's always been a risk-taker, she boasts. It's part of her success, part of her drive. "I think the personal risks I take are enormous," she says. That's why Linda Ronstadt is always a woman for surprise and change.

7

There's no denying that men and Linda Ronstadt are inextricably linked. And the pattern was set early on, as she confesses. "Ever since I was six years old," she claims, "I've been looking for the perfect boyfriend." And, revealing further memories of a boy-crazed childhood, she says, "I was boy crazy in the first grade. Still am."

But Linda has had her troubles with men. The heartbreak she sings so plaintively of in her songs has a real basis. She's had a string of broken romances behind her, and a heart, she claims, bruised and battered. She's unwisely mixed career and love and has wound up suffering on both accounts because of it. Then, too, just her intense sexual vibes are enough to spark off rumors linking her with any man she's seen with. Linda despairs about the talk but figures that that's just part of the normal fallout when you're a celebrity of that magnitude.

But there is an unmistakable tension between her professional life and her personal life. Linda never seems to waver on the subject of marriage

and states flatly that her freedom and the demands of the road are more important to her than a husband. And her iconoclastic, restless way of life also rules out the possibility of marriage. Tellingly, part of her song repertoire is the Dolly Parton classic, *I Never Will Marry*. As she says, "At first I didn't get married because I was busy getting my career going. Then it was because I hadn't seen enough of the world. I thought I might meet the man in England, for example. I treated it like shopping for shoes. Now I realize I didn't get married because I just didn't want to. My mobility was more important. As the years have passed, I've come to feel that maybe I never will get married."

That doesn't bother her, nor is it some kind of rationalization for her romantic life filled with such ups and downs. Linda says she might like one steady and serious relationship, but then adds with a typically whimsical grin that she's also curious enough to have more than one relationship in her lifetime. She feels that being involved with many men keeps her open and makes her learn more.

"It has been a real education to me not to have gotten married because it's meant I can take up with all different kinds of people. I really learn so much that way. But you don't get anything without paying the price for it. You can get a lot of wounds from going through relationships. You can eventually get to where you never really would trust anyone enough to give your heart away completely."

Most of the men in her life have been musicians, which is expected for someone so prominent in the rock world. She attempts, she claims, to stay away from romantic liaisons with her sidemen on the road. But it's not always easy to abide by that maxim, especially since Linda is frequently the only woman on the road. She also adds with a wily note in her voice that sometimes the situation can get intriguing if she's traveling with another group.

And yet much of the pain and ache she feels is exactly because of her entanglements with musicians. For one thing, she explains that getting involved with someone in your own field makes natural competitiveness arise. The problem with living with a musician, as Linda says more than once, is that inevitably jealousies come out and tensions erupt because of conflicting schedules and differences in media profiles. It would be hard, after all, for a fellow mucician to live with Linda Ronstadt and not be threatened by her towering reputation.

Then again, living with a man who is not a musician can be equally problematic. He's only able to get the bare leftovers of her time after she's through with the touring and the recording and the rehearsing,

which can amount to some five per cent.

What does Linda do? Now she says she is "learning to live alone," but it wasn't always that way. At the beginning stages of her career, she spent her time on and off stage with men who doubled as lovers and managers. Linda just didn't want to be alone; she needed the guidance of a man, she felt. It wasn't particularly smart, but Linda was much younger then and much more vulnerable than she is today. She felt the need of some kind of father-figure to watch over her, make her decisions for her, take care of her.

And also what she needed, during that time of turbulent decision-making, was someone she felt was on her side. She needed someone to root for her in the production arena, and didn't feel strong enough to be left to her own devices.

John Boylan was one of the first men who played a dual professional and personal role in her life. Linda is candid enough to admit that her romance with him was pretty much of a "dad-kid relationship" as she likes to say.

"I'd wake up and call and ask, 'Gee, what should I do today? What socks should I put on?' " She regrets that her lack of confidence then was enough to make her seek a father-figure who would tell her what to do.

J. D. Souther is a songwriter and a producer that Linda is still relatively friendly with today. He still writes songs for her to record. Linda once giggled when she received one of his albums, kissed the record and said, demurely, "My one love." With Souther, she worked long and hard hours in the studio, hours which were grueling but Linda liked being with him.

"I started re-recording everything with J. D. Souther. We were like kids in the studio, just inept, and we took a lot of time. But I learned a lot and it was worth it, almost, because it was such hard work. After that experience, I knew so much more when I went into the studio, it wasn't like I was a person who didn't know how to do what she wanted to do."

But despite the studio benefits, Linda came away from all these confused relationships with more than a bit of ambivalence about men. It's not that she doesn't want them, it's just that it's so hard to keep a relationship going and growing and at the same time, keep it from killing you.

As Linda once said, "You never know what will happen if you get involved with somebody. ... I mean a relationship could be the worst thing that's ever happened, ya know? It could be the worst thing that happened in their career. Or my career. It's so weird, since we all live in fishbowls it's so difficult to have successful relationships."

Being a singer like she is only complicated matters, Linda knows. She talks about how being in show business robs you of the emotional security and stability necessary for a more permanent relationship. And she says that it can make you paranoid and volatile because people in the public eye are liked for a myriad of reasons and sometimes the reasons have nothing to do with who they are and what they're like inside, underneath the glamour and the glitter.

Some people do treat her like Linda Ronstadt, she confesses, instead of just being Linda. But those people didn't stay around because Linda says the situation was just too "uncomfortable". It's the people who are very sure of themselves and who regard her as just another person whom Linda feels the closest to.

But, as Linda became more confident in her work and more faithful in herself, she ended her period of paternal, watch-man type relationships with men who told her what to do and how to do it. And she started, perhaps not so coincidentally, making more solid friendships with women. As she became less of a clinging vine vamp and a more self-

assured person, she probably felt less threatened by women and grew closer to them. And her strength of course showed through in her music. The turning point really came when Linda broke up with someone during the making of *Don't Cry Now*, which significantly was a real musical breakthrough for her.

"I had just broken up with someone I was living with. The relationship had been real oppressive to me. It had lasted a long time and created a lot of fear in my music. He was a musician too. After we broke up, I seemed to make a lot of friends all of a sudden. I met Emmylou Harris Washington and she turned me on to a lot of people."

Now Linda remains fairly philosophical about romance and relationships. She's finally come to terms with the fact that she's single and has stopped apologizing for it. And she's accepted the fact that her career makes certain requirements so that she can't have it all. Physical proof of this is when she toted around an article in the Village Voice about a woman living alone and enjoying her lifestyle. That was another trigger which helped Linda form closer relationships with women. As her relationships with men have become more mature and less scattered, so have her relationships with women flowered. It's as if Linda is enjoying her womanhood and her selfhood, and her travails with romance are really just another aspect of her struggles with self-discovery. The floundering, the mishaps and the mistakes with men were all part of that search.

Now she says she has lots of boyfriends, instead of having just one. She tries to get her sense of security from herself and not from a man. Critics who accuse Linda of depending and leaning on Asher can be refuted by the fact that it's not the sexlessness of their relationship that makes things different. It's also the fact that Linda, while subscribing to Peter's fine talents, also feels strong enough to assert herself and make her opinions be heard. When she was maintaining a lover-producer relationship, she couldn't do that.

Now Linda has discovered that it's not so horrible to wake up in the mornings alone. She thinks, "I can read," or do any number of other activities. And as she progresses in her search for self-discovery outside linking up with a man, she finds that she has much more in common with other women singers than she used to think. And she's similarly found that she has more ability to relate to other women outside the music industry.

"It used to be that girl singers were the only professional women I knew. All my women friends encourage and support each other. Mostly

we're all single and we find that we're enjoying it."

Life at the top can be decidedly lonely, confesses the sexy girl who projects such an aura of abandon and come-hither vibrations when she performs. The intense sexuality creates rumors that she has a more active life romantically than she does have. She is fond of cracking, "I keep saying I wish I had as much in bed as I get in the papers. I'd be real busy."

But still, Linda does little to quell the talk, when she performs on stage in a tight hot pants outfit and high heels, the kind of clothes that she says brings out what she likes to call her "hooker streak".

But she gets upset that all the talk about whom she's dating and going around with can get in the way of her music, and the most important thing, that terrific voice. She frets that the romantic gossip detracts from the vocal talent. And it is certainly an undeniable fact that who Linda Ronstadt might be seeing at any given moment is almost as exciting to people as the power of her singing. But the way she delivers her songs makes it seem like Linda's life is very much a part of the performance.

"I've always liked to flirt," admits Linda. "That's fun. But that element has been overemphasized. I don't want it to overshadow the music or other elements in my personality. That's not all there is to me."

But Linda's conspicuous image as a teaser and a flirt can get very uncomfortable for her to handle. She uses the work "devoured" a lot when she speaks of the gossip and talks about wanting to hide to keep her privacy. And she doesn't relish the position of being such a highly-charged sexual being. She will talk with some concern that many people are nervous about being seen with her because of this much-touted picture of her as a "carousing rock 'n' roller".

For example, a picture of Linda being introduced to Carl Bernstein spun off a whole series of rumours about a supposed romance with him several years ago, before his marriage to writer Nora Ephron. Linda was not very happy about that, especially since it was the one and only time she had ever met him. And another time, a picture of Linda with Peter Asher, the manager with whom she has loudly proclaimed to the world not to be her lover, was garnished with the caption that the two of them were househunting, in Malibu. At the time, Linda already owned a house in Malibu and Peter was very much married to one of her favorite girlfriends.

And she once grimly joked about a photo that was taken of her with her dog in her backyard, without her permission, "It's just a good thing my dog is female or God only knows what they'd be writing."

Curiously, despite her frequent policy of maintaining multiple

boyfriends, instead of leading a one-man, one-woman lifestyle, Linda insists that women are "by nature more inclined to be monogamous". Her statement may not ring any choruses of acclaim from feminists but she insists that it's part of her belief system.

She knows that she herself has had many lovers in her lifetime so there is a bit of contradiction in that statement. But actually, she maintains that her life is set up for just one man, and that a woman with a career is in a situation that is difficult to deal with as far as romantic entanglements go.

Linda once discussed how she was intrigued by the concept of the geisha girl and her supreme independence and cultivation in so many areas. She likened the geisha's role to her own situation, as far as her many talents and her relationship to men. In contrast, Linda feels, the

role of the wife is that of a stable and steady figurehead. There are two paths, she thinks, open to women today; either to pursue that of the geisha or that of the wife. And Linda certainly doesn't want to be a wife.

But she really doesn't consider herself cast in the mold of a geisha either. As she says, lightheartedly, "The trouble with being a latter-day geisha is that those geishas could really do it. ... I'm only a half-assed geisha. I can only sing."

Clearly, Linda is struggling with the role of a liberated and healthy sexual woman today. She likes men and is a flirt, but she doesn't want that to be the extent of her personality. It's a fine and hard line to tread between being fulfilled physically and being fulfilled as a person.

For a while that fulfillment took the form of trying relationships with other professional types besides musicians. She lived for a while with comedian Albert Brooks and a friend named Adam Mitchell, with whom her relationship was totally platonic. But even those relationships didn't lead to perfection.

"Men give you a nasty choice," she claims. "Either you put up with them chipping away at you emotionally or you don't have them. Well, I've chosen not to have them—not to live with someone. I chose to have lots of boyfriends instead of one, and I look to myself for my own security."

Linda's reputation is certainly colored with vivid and often exaggerated tales of her supposed promiscuity. She claims of course that much of it is all hype, and she also says that that doesn't mean she has to fall in love with every guy she goes to bed with. What she says she'd like is to have a relationship with warmth and tenderness and kindness and affection. There would be the physical element too of course, but it doesn't have to be love. But that doesn't mean it can't be a viable relationship.

"I'm always looking," says Linda. But she realizes that that might be the way it will be for her for the rest of her life, that the search may be more important to her than the finding of it. And she kind of enjoys being forever on the prowl—it suits her restless image. She also realizes that she may never have children but that doesn't seem to bother her either.

As she told Rolling Stone, "I think the fact that I haven't met a man that I want to have children with has prevented me from having children. The thing I thought most about was that if I did get married and have children and it was too comfortable for me, it would take away my desire."

Having children, Linda says, might be a ready excuse for her not to do the things she's frightened of doing, like going out on tour or recording. And she worries that having a family might make her develop a kind of inertia that would paralyze her career. It represents to Linda what she calls a "big gamble, a big risk". But she feels it's also kind of a debatable issue since she doesn't really know anybody that she would like to have a family with.

She calls her lifestyle one of drifting, and although that would bother some people, it wouldn't bother her. The idea that she may drift for the rest of her life has occurred to her but it doesn't faze her. She seems to be able to foresee her life as a series of falling in and out of love with a variety of people, all of whom contribute to her personal growth. Linda may have been cheated and bruised in the past, but it constitutes the whole package that is so well known as Linda Ronstadt.

One of the loose-styled relationships Linda has had was with Mick Jagger, the charismatic lead singer of the Rolling Stones. Like Linda, Mick is probably one of the rock world's most publicized stars and his romantic peccadilloes are as famous as the variety of women he's been with. At first their relationship was one of more or less professional counseling, as Mick gave Linda a clearer perspective on her performing style. He had come backstage to see her one night in London and advised her to sing more rock and fewer ballads because it was rock that he felt was her strong point.

As a result of Mick's suggestion, Linda started doing a rambunctious, boisterous rock number that was one of the Stones repertoire called *Tumbling Dice*. She likes the way people respond to the song, the way they bounced in their seats and really move to the music. It became one of those magical, charismatic Ronstadt numbers that really showed off her voice to advantage.

When Linda likes a man, she likes him with almost unbounded, unalloyed enthusiasm. There's no middle ground for her. Thus, in her praise of Mick, she complimented his strength and his shrewd intelligence and she admired his powerful stance in the rock world. Linda and Mick palled around a lot in London when she was performing there. But, like with many other men, Linda found that she was wary with him. She speaks of him as being what she calls "dangerous", alluding to his demonish streak and his penchant for some naughty ways. Linda says, "He's as bad as they say and as good."

Mick, says Linda, has a kind of dangerously entrancing orbit that can sort of carry you in like a tidal wave or a quagmire. In other words, Mick,

ever the restless womanizer, can have you all tied up over him and then collapse as he becomes bored and decides to hunt for other pastures. He's an enticing figure but one that can obviously be hurtful as well as beneficial.

Linda's most current and most mysterious romance is with a political figure. The man is none other than the Governor of California, the staid and reclusive Jerry Brown, recently re-elected for his second term as governor, and cited as prime Presidential timber for the next election in 1980.

It's no accident that Linda has become involved with someone from the political arena. Most politicians are as intrigued with the people of glamorous show business as the powers that be in government are as attractive to people in the entertainmnent world. As Linda became a much more prominent rock personality and her reputation expanded, she became close to many political figures, such as political activist and campaigner, Tom Hayden, who is also the husband of Jane Fonda, and Chip Carter, which resulted in her appearance at President Carter's Inaugural Ball.

It also came about because of a kind of exploratory venture on Linda's part. After one of her tours, and feeling that she had confined herself too much to the music world for her interests and her men, she decided to expand her sights. What she did, she explains, was "cruise around and look at all kinds of lives. I met astronauts, TV people, doctors, politicians. I discovered there was something more to life than the music business and different kinds of men than musicians. I used to think they were only the kinds of men I could get involved with. ... Now I know they aren't the most trustworthy lot."

But whether Jerry is the kind of person that Linda considers trustworthy, one thing that the public finds about him is that he is an exceedingly confusing figure. He's a unique type of politician who shuns the glamorous fringe benefits of the government life. His role as governor entitled him to live in an opulent governor's home yet Jerry Brown passes up the mansion and had the state limousine and plane put into storage. Brown not only is a puzzling figure, he talks in puzzles. Sometimes his speeches and conversations are threaded with Zen sayings or spoutings of philosophy. Brown, a confirmed bachelor, or at least up until he met Linda, spent three and a half years of his life in a Jesuit seminary. Then he left the seminarian's life in 1960 to pursue a legal career. He studied at Berkeley and Yale Law School and then he went to Los Angeles to practice. He right away established himself as a liberal-

Heading for the White House
Linda and her No. 1 man, Gov. Jerry Brown of California.

minded politician, working against the war in Vietnam and supporting Senator Eugene McCarthy in his presidential campaign. Then he became governor and his ascent to political prominence was indubitably helped by the fact that his father had also served as governor of California, Edmund G. Pat Brown.

Like Linda, Jerry remains pretty much a bachelor guy. He has to continually deny that he and Linda are getting married or that they've eloped, and insists that he has no plans to marry Linda or anyone. Recently the Wall Street Journal and Rona Barrett both reported stories that Jerry and Linda would wed soon, but he squelched the rumors right away. He speaks of vague marital ambitions, but in the next breath talks about how his ever-growing political ambition would be too harmful to a wife and family.

The romance between the politico and the rock queen began in Lucy's El Adobe, a Mexican restaurant in Los Angeles, where they met for the first time. They discovered that although from apparently different and striking worlds, there were also many bonds between them. Both were Catholic, both were public figures dogged by the press and photographers and both were familiar with the toll taken by traveling on the road.

Linda quickly offered her support to the Governor by singing at a benefit concert for him in 1976, to raise money for his Presidential campaign. Their closeness began to grow. Careful to avoid the photographers and the newsmen, Linda and Jerry Brown started to go out publicly, to such places as a tribute to playwright Neil Simon and a reception at the Beverly Wilshire Hotel. They also frequented such places as the Roxy in Los Angeles. And they spent Christmas together. Linda was accompanied by Jerry to his hometown of San Francisco, where he gave her a specially guided tour. And he claims to use her house in Malibu as a sanctuary which is why his car is parked over there so much of the time—or at least that's the way Jerry cleverly puts it.

He came right out and admitted as much when he defended an action he took during the rain storms in March of 1978. The National Guard was summoned, under his orders, to sandbag her house to prevent it from sliding into the sea. When Californians protested such a display of what they called blatant nepotism, the governor defended his action by saying that he considered Linda's home a sanctuary. His aides, in the same vein, reported that Jerry likes it there because it's safe and secluded and well-guarded—so much so that he can relax there.

But despite this public admission that Governor Brown was indeed

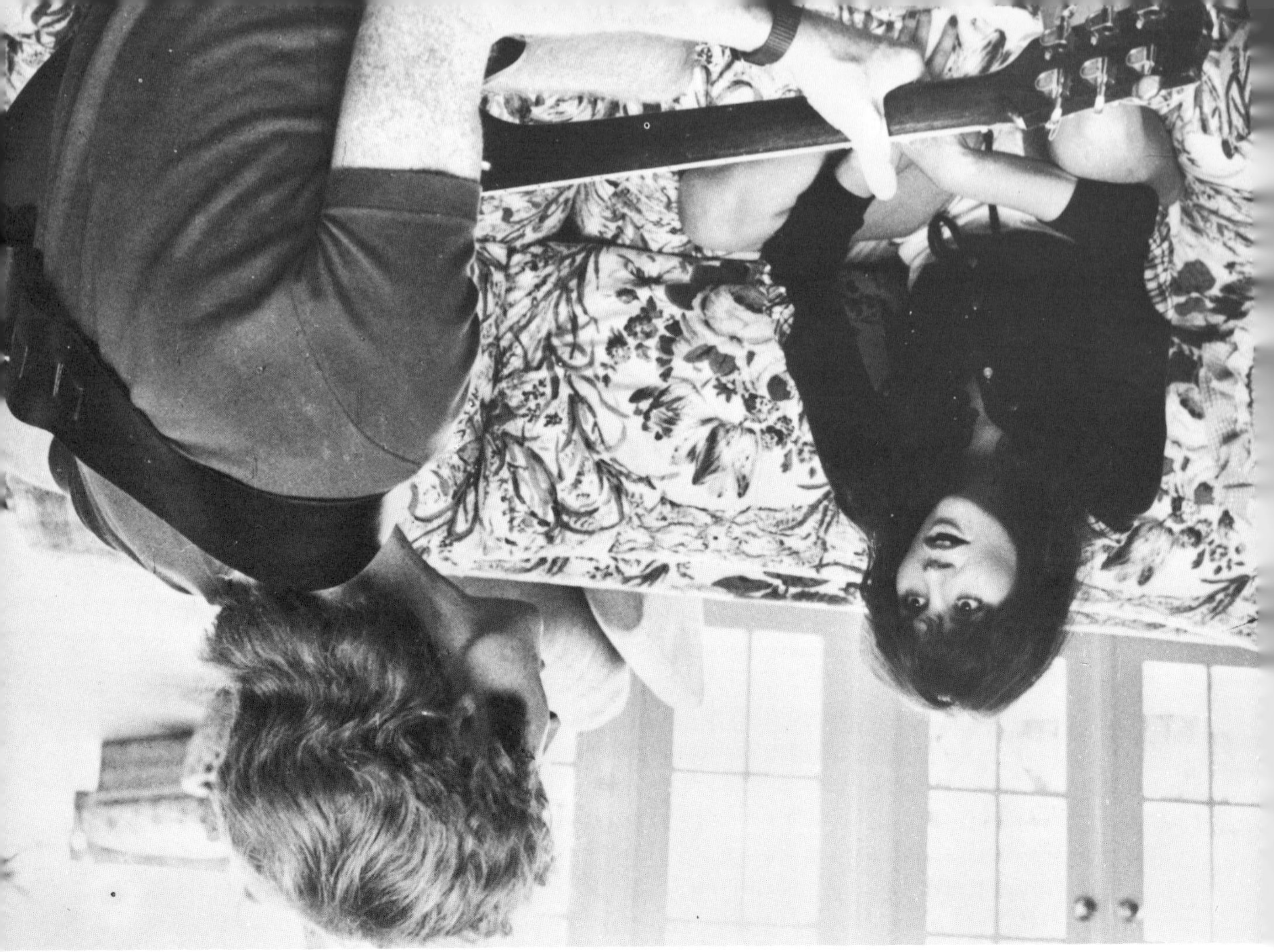

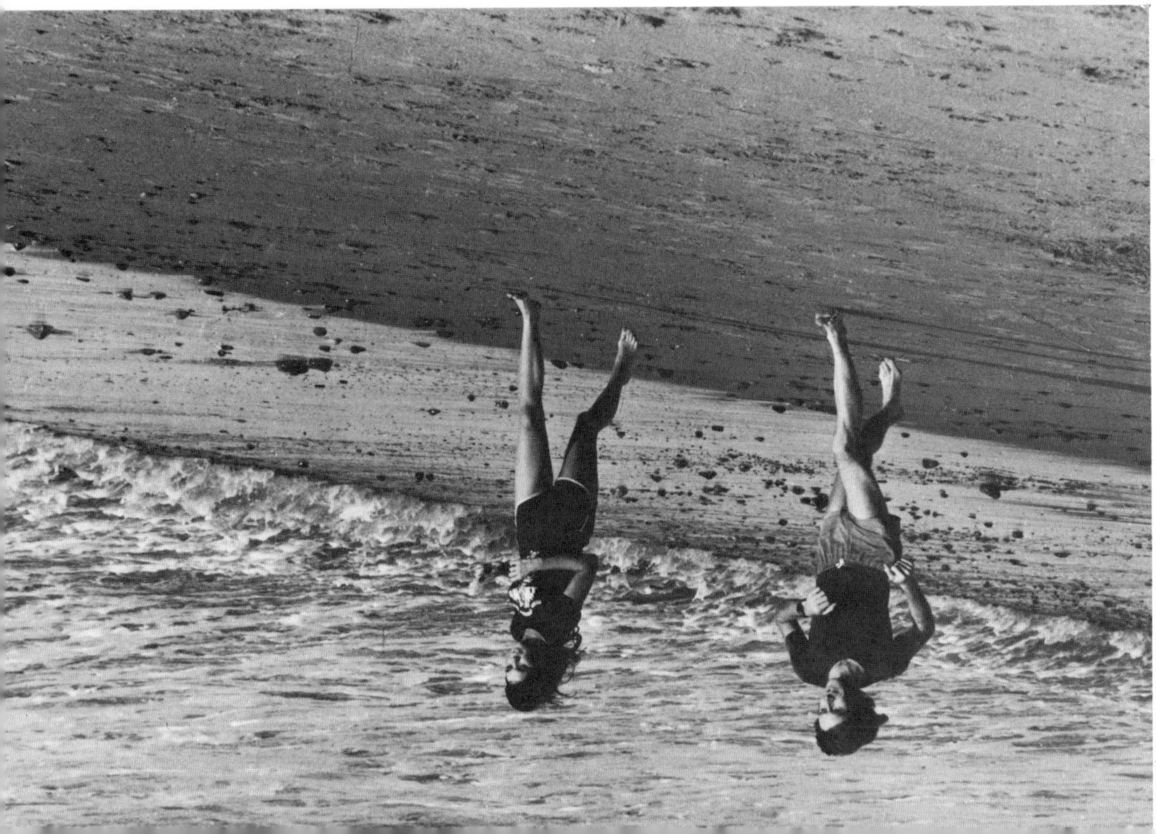

racking up quite a few hours at the home of Linda Ronstadt, their romance has been decidedly undercover. Linda, always loathsome towards publicity, does not like to talk about her relationship with Jerry and he is equally quiet. Photos of them together are absolutely impossible to obtain; usually what a zealous photographer winds up with is a shot of Linda rushing out to a car with a book in front of her face or a coat over her head. And they further frustrate the press by arriving and leaving in separate cars whenever they go somewhere.

Neither of them has any specific reasons for maintaining such low profiles about their romance. The voters have expressed opinions for the most part, that reveal it would make no difference to them if Jerry Brown remains a bachelor or gets married. And while in more conservative states the idea of a governor linked with a rock star would cause more than a little alarm, in liberal-minded California, where the citizens are used to the most aberrant state of affairs, Jerry's liaison with Linda is taken without any shock.

But the spark of interest about Jerry and Linda is whether their relationship is platonic or more than that. In the book Brown, by writer Orville Schell, it is described how the author arrives at the Malibu sanctuary only to be greeted by a sleepy-eyed Linda, followed by the governor. The three discussed that day whether Linda should accompany them to a train ride with a delegation of Chinese. And in another episode, Schell talked about how the three of them were crammed into the Porsche Linda owned, with the rock star demurely perched on Jerry Brown's lap.

That does sound like there's something more than platonic cooking between the two but other observers of Linda and Jerry disagree. They insist that Linda is just as close with Brown as ever but simply as a friend. Brown, they say, appreciates the privacy he has when he's at her house. Another man who wrote a book on Brown similarly felt that Jerry wouldn't have a serious relationship with Linda because of her checkered romantic past, strewn with so many men. But while there's a lot of speculation going on, there is not much tangible truth to hang on to. And that's obviously the way Linda and Jerry want it. Whatever the parameters of their relationship, it is certainly noticed by even the press. That's why Rolling Stone magazine gave Jerry Brown its groupie of the year award in 1977, a claim of dubious distinction.

Whether the future of Jerry Brown, which he hopes will include the Presidency, will also include Linda Ronstadt in the permanent picture is uncertain. The two are close now but Washington, D.C. is a scrupulous

and more strait-laced city than Linda and Jerry are used to. The demands of society there are far more rigid. It would be hard for the doyennes of Washington to accept Linda as their first lady. And, as much as Linda complains about the fishbowl life of Hollywood now, she'd be under even more scrutiny if she lived in Washington. It's difficult to imagine Linda in that role.

But right now, marriage is far from Linda's mind. She's more interested in setting up a security system inside herself. She feels happier, more content than she has in ages, and that's probably because the array of destructive relationships are all in the past and Linda is very much in control of her life. A certain core of strength is emerging out of her. She no longer feels the need to cling to a man for advice or for identity.

Of course she's battling loneliness, but that's something she can learn to cope with. The days on the road are the worst. She confesses to a kind

of aching feeling when she has to head back to her hotel room all alone. She really doesn't want to pick up some guy and invite him back to her room with her. It's a problem voiced by many female singers who tour the country and Linda is not unique in this way.

Because, as Linda points out, sometimes when you live with somebody you can get even lonelier. If you latch on to somebody just to live with him, then that can be the loneliest state of all.

The use and disabuse she sings of so mournfully in her songs are pretty much in the past. It's not indicative of the present-day Linda who is less willing to let men take advantage of her. As she puts it, "People don't blow me out of the water the way they used to."

It looks like Linda's got the situation between her and men all worked out and no more cheating or mistreating will come her way.

In 1978, Linda Ronstadt finally made it to the movies, appropriately enough in a film about the hectic world of radio programming called FM. The movies centered around the big music phenomenon of the late 1960's and early 1970's, in which the popular sounds of the day started to be played and heard over the FM air waves, formerly reserved for the more staid, Muzak-type tunes and softer, blander offerings. One important thing about the character of the new FM station which spun popular records—there were fewer commercial interruptions than on their AM counterparts.

The film FM started exactly with that premise—a hip station called QSKY in Los Angeles, one of the more highly-rated in the town, was being threatened with too much commercialization by the big bosses. The people who ran the station felt an altruistic and genuine responsibility to their audiences to not allow this profit-blind motive to ruin their programs, almost totally free of commercial advertisement.

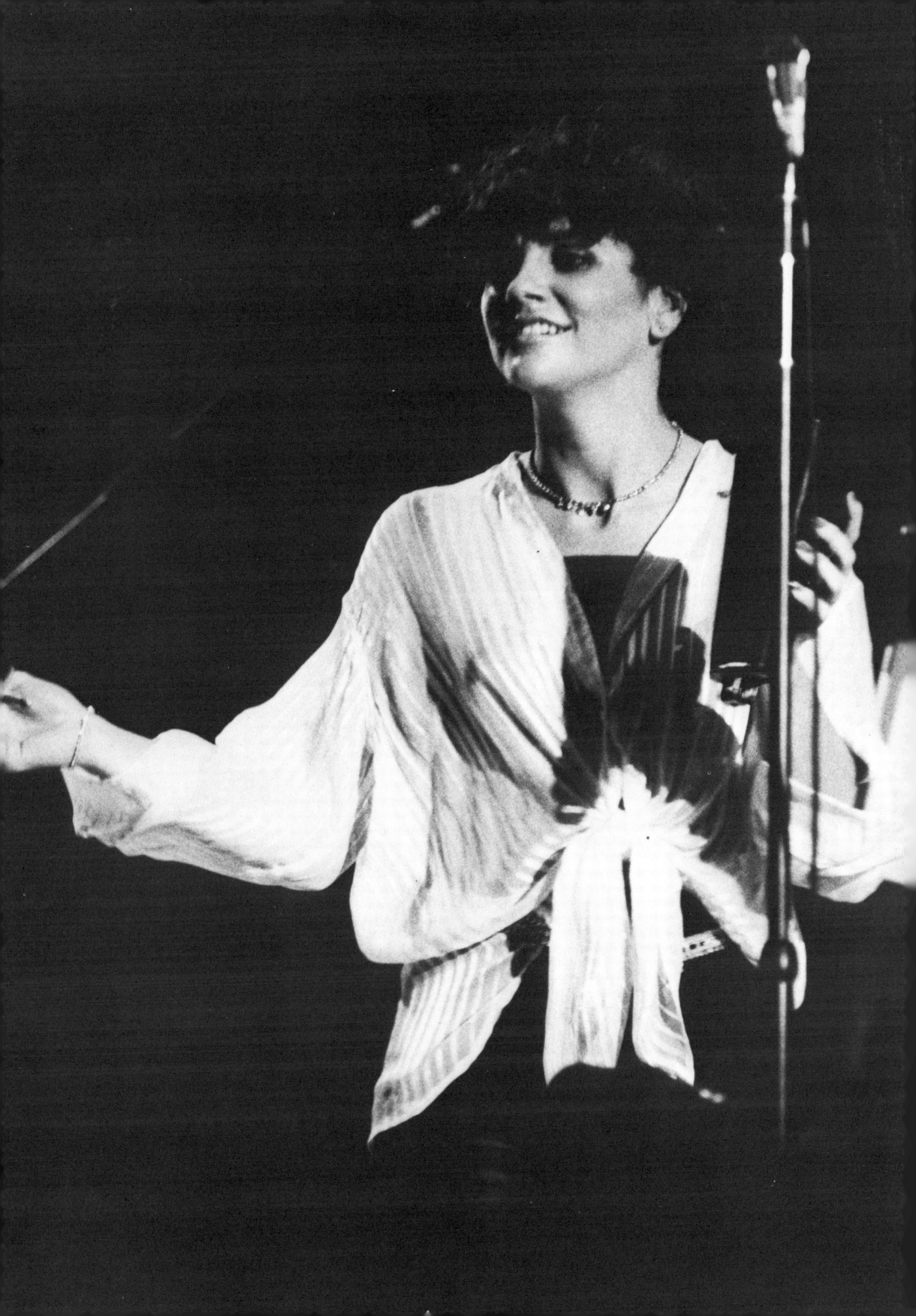

But money and visions of increased revenue do not always go hand in hand with for-the-people attitudes. So a struggle ensued, flared particularly by the refusal of the station to play jingles promoting the new fun Army. What eventually happens is that the conscientious radio station workers go on strike, protesting the greed of their corporate and hypocritical bosses. At the climax of the film, in the midst of the strike, the much-adored station manager, played by Michael Brandon, makes a poignant plea for sanity and brotherhood. He says that the strikers will give up, but that they will also give the audience what it hopes to get, if not from this station, then from somewhere else. At this point the dour boss behind the whole trouble steps forward, obviously moved by this unalloyed integrity of the radio station corps. He vows to let them go on and do their thing, regardless of the loss of profits. And so, on this saccharine note, ends the story of FM, a movie predictable in plot and a Hollywood attempt to build a more or less nothing movie around some good rock songs.

Linda played herself, doing what she would be expected to do, singing in a rock concert. For those who had only seen her before in a stage from a far-off seat in the middle of one of those large rock concert stadiums, it was a chance to see Linda, vibrant and sexy and alive, up close. She even dressed up for the part—or at least not so casual as she usually does for concert romps. No Cub Scout uniform this time, instead, she donned a loose-fitting blouse tied at the waist with a scarf at the neck. She also wore form-hugging pants tucked into boots. There was a smile on her face—none of the uptight Linda in this film—and a flower in her hair. She looked like she was enjoying the movie making process.

She sings three songs. First is the raucous Mick Jagger-Keith Richard composition called *Tumbling Dice*. It's done in a demure style, with modest and quiet jumps and shakes, not the outrageous way Linda would do it if she were truly emulating Mick. Next comes the soulful and black-humored tune by Warren Zevon called *Poor, Poor Pitiful Me*, which so stimulates and excites the audience that at the conclusion they jump to their feet and clamor for more. But first Linda, obviously in character, expresses her thanks to the station manager and station QSKY for the broadcast. Then she launches into her finale, the haunting Elvis Presley ballad called *Love Me Tender*. The demeanor she assumes is much different for this song than for her previous ones. She's much quieter, more thoughtful and more poignant. Waddy Wachtel, the guitar player in her band, harmonizes along with Linda on this song.

Linda's performance was one of the high points in what was otherwise

a very mediocre and limp movie. The script was called by some critics "dopey," and it seems that the actors have very little to do. But the acute acting ability of people like Michael Brandon, in the role of the station manager, Eileen Brennan as the obligatory, sultry-voiced siren over the air waves at night and Martin Mull, playing a Ted Knight-like talk show host really saves the movie.

Eileen Brennan, called "Mother" in the film, evokes laughs from the audience just from the unbelievable exaggerated quality of her rasping voice. Alex Karras, who has appeared in Blazing Saddles, enacts the part of an aging disc jockey.

But perhaps the most enjoyable performance of all belongs to Martin Mull, who is delightfully and insufferably pompous and vain. He's the kind of person who's so repulsive he becomes attractive because of it. Coincidentally, Martin used to be a rock star, but then found fame as the much-adored star of Mary Hartman, Mary Hartman and Fernwood 2-Night.

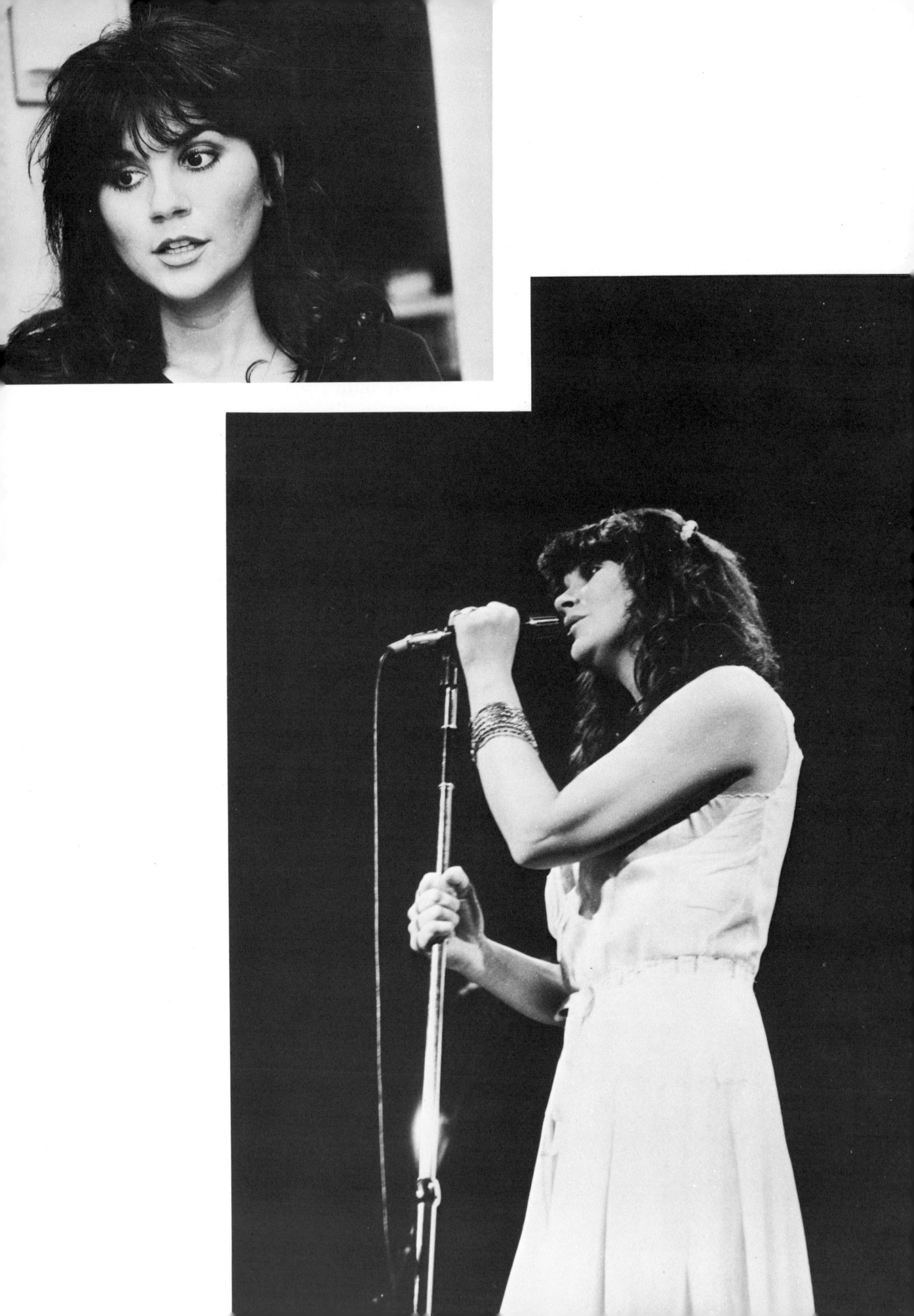

Also rounding out the cast are Cleavon Little, as the disc jockey called Prince of Darkness and Cassie Yates as the attractive disc jockey called Laura Coe.

One of the liveliest moments in the film comes when Martin and Brandon clash in a kind of mock battle. There is so much sensitivity and earnestness thrown around that the tenor of the fight is almost laughable. At the end of the battle, Mull dissolves into tears and dolefully sucks his thumb.

Apparently, Linda felt that her concert appearance in the movie was enough for the film-making process. She didn't really want to get that involved with the movie after it was out, and had veto power as far as publicity photos for the film were concerned. Maybe Linda felt that she just about tuned out on FM after the movie was made. In any case, she did not go out of her way to promote it or publicize it.

9

She does seem to have it all, Linda Ronstadt, this high-charged queen of rock, commanding the respect and admiration of thousands and millions of rock fans all over the country. But there is a continually elusive quality about her life that obviously troubles her and that is her lack of what she prefers to call "Domestic bliss."

As she told Redbook, "The price I pay for my lifestyle is not being able to have domesticity. Domestic bliss must be the highest form of bliss a human being can experience. I have profound respect for it. A woman who can do it all involves and have a career is really the exception."

But as she's learned to muster the strength and the inner stability, she finds that being alone—which translated means being without a man—doesn't have to be that bad. Her social life for the most part revolves around the men in her band and their wives, and their girlfriends, her manager and the three women who work for her, a trio that is comprised of a housekeeper, a secretary, and the foreman of her house. Linda finds

these relationships a great source of sustenance and relief in her lonely lifestyle.

Her life now seems to be a curious combination of flux and stability. There is the constancy of her relationships with friends and crew and her home. But there is also the flux of new men and the traveling lifestyle on the road which will never become easy for someone as basically shy and queasy before the voracious public as she is.

Musically of course the trend has always been clear. Linda, even judged by the severest of critics, keeps getting better and expanding her repertoire all the time. She's branched out from the realm of rock into blues and soul and straight ballads and even more demanding numbers out of the customary pop singer's fare. Even her astute manager, Peter Asher, cannot predict exactly where Linda will go, what she will do in the next few years. That is undoubtedly because her possibility is endless.

"I think she will write more. She will continue to do her stuff," he muses. Linda, ever-modest, says, "I'm feeling around." And she's thus exploring the worlds of reggae, Bulgarian ballads, third world tunes and other esoteric kinds of music. She wants to keep changing and keep doing more than she's done before. And it's not only musically that she's experiencing growth. She's also enlarging her interests through, a more intellectually-oriented caliber of friends and wide-ranging interests outside the music world. For Linda, growth means more than in just the musical areas. It means enlargement of her entire personality, and it's clear that she's been working on that kind of achievement ever since she left Arizona to go to Hollywood.

But, inevitably, there is still the confusion and the torment and the uncertainty and that's what Linda is learning how to deal with better than before. The bewilderment is still there but she's learning how to handle it better and how to muddle through the periods when she feels besieged by the tremendous responsibilities of someone in her position.

There are times, she admits, when she feels that her nerves just won't be able to take the pressure and then things get better and she figures, "Hey, this is great. I've got it all figured out. I'm never giving up."

What she has also figured out is that she is invariably on the edge of discontent and unhappiness, and that it is in fact this malaise that has spurred her on to other things and helped her reach new heights in her career. She does not appear particularly happy or pleased with her phenomenal achievements, but instead reckons that once something is done, there's a new level to achieve, a higher demand to be met. She is almost the classic case of the star who is chronically and forever displeased

Linda runs through a couple of songs for her album Simple Dreams before the long studio sessions begin.

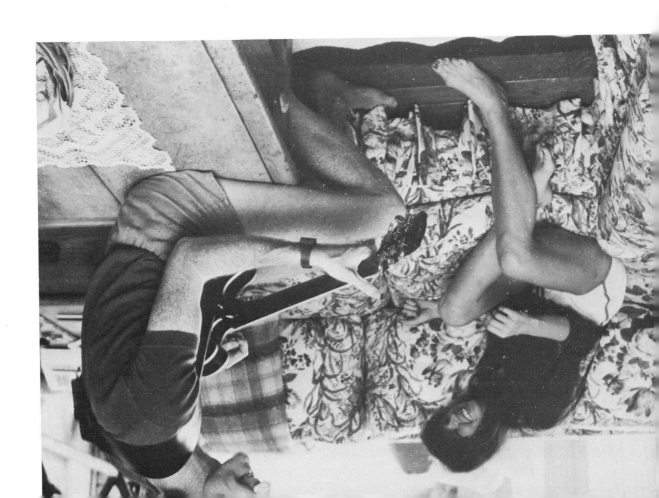

with herself. In a sense it is true that Linda Ronstadt has everything and yet the spiritual and intangible things that really matter, she doesn't seem to be able to get within her grasp at all.

She is the first to realize and verbalize this. She says, "At some point I ceased thinking I was unhappy because I didn't become more successful or that success would make me happier. I realized that after a while. And at that point, I thought there was no hope ever. I realized I would just struggle forever."

And so she continues to struggle, although her struggle is in more Herculean terms than most of us deal with. She struggles to maintain her level of stardom, to experiment without risking a badly embarrassing failure, to top previous levels of achievement. The dilemma is obvious. What can you do to surprise and startle when you're a star of Linda's magnitude? Where do you go when you're at the top? What happens next to the queen of rock?

Not surprisingly, although she is silent and mysterious about the topic, she confesses that she contemplates getting back to something out of the show business realm altogether. When asked by a Rolling Stone reporter what she thought she would be doing in five years, she replied that she didn't know. But she immediately brought up the subject of falling in love, which appears to be something that bothers her. And then she went on to say how she thinks about cutting back, simply producing less, and then just pursuing other avenues than the one she's so far along on now of rock star. It wouldn't be movies but it might be something totally startling to those who have adored Linda on her musical pedestal.

Yes, she admits, she has mulled over the possibility of not making records at all at some point and rather getting into something as far off afield as farming. The point is that Linda just doesn't know what she'll be doing next and she doesn't want to be pinned down.

What would make Linda jump down from her place at the zenith of rock? For one thing, she complains about her feelings that rock and roll contributes to a kind of what she calls continued adolescence—a kind of teen attitude that is fostered by the glitter and the groupies and the fans and the appearances. Now that Linda is concentrating on her head growth, she doesn't want to keep within that framework anymore.

Although it's an arduous process, making records is something Linda genuinely enjoys. But the complementary and necessary aspect that troubles her is touring and she'll never get accustomed to that. But as long as she makes records, she'll be forced to tour. It's a simple fact of the music business—to sell records, you have to tour to promote and sell

Linda Ronstadt: celebrity . . .

them. But she freely admits that making records is far more preferable to her than performing on stage.

What does she want out of life—simply what everyone else wants and perhaps more basic things than most. She who has so much success and money and fame says, "The most important thing to do is something that's satisfying and something you do well and that you enjoy doing. If you're doing that it doesn't matter."

One thing that is of prime importance to Linda in the future is to enjoy herself and try to attain some happiness. She recently went to Europe, not on tour, but on vacation with her mother. When she cruised aboard the Queen Elizabeth II with her mother, she had thought she was getting away from it all—no such luck, however, as she grew irate when a baggage man insisted she was Linda Ronstadt the rock star. When Linda denied it, the man quipped that either she was a liar or else she was stealing Linda Ronstadt's luggage. So, Linda admitted who she was.

Time and again, Linda has been asked if she subconsciously chose a profession in which it would be difficult if not impossible to have some kind of domestic stability. After all, how many female rock stars are happily married—other than Carly Simon and Rita Coolidge. She maintains instead that she just sings well and that she gravitated toward music naturally when as a child she urged her parents to "Play me some music." So there's her profession and the fact that she's attracted to men who are in the music business and similarly rootless in a sense and her lifestyle. But she didn't choose music as a way out of a steady relationship. "Whatever I started singing for ... it makes you feel good."

Linda looks forward, ironically for many people in show business, to getting older, because with the advancing of years she finds that she has become wiser and more in control. She believes, she says, that age gives you more facts and more of a perspective and that helps a lot.

Part of that added perspective she hopes to continue to hone by traveling—like she did this summer with her mother—to all kinds of places. She'd like to venture into the Third World countries, perhaps to pick up some musical idioms along the way. The traveling, the broadening of interests, she feels, might help her gain some new feelings for her music. She's also working on learning a few instruments, toying a bit with the guitar and vowing to learn to play the piano someday. And then of course there is that move to New York which represents not only a geographical distancing from her old ways and modes of life but also kind of a symbol of being recharged and rejuvenated for the future.

Unlike the lyrics of the golden oldies, rock and roll, for Linda Ronstadt, is not here to stay. She's heading toward softer and more subdued kinds of music. "I want some grace and dignity in my old age," she quips. She talks about becoming somewhat of a chanteuse or cabaret singer, as opposed to the very youthful and in some senses confining rock and roll bit. As Linda metamorphoses into more of a woman, so goes her music. As she shed the teeny-bopper and kid-like image, so does she shed the kind of one-sided powerful rock numbers she's been so famous for in the past. Change for Linda means change all around. She is not a person apart from her music.

The pitfalls may be there, the ups and downs and mood vicissitudes may forever plague her, but things are getting better for Linda and the future, always promising, looks personally more optimistic, even from her cynical and somewhat jaundiced point of view. "What's different now," she says with a sly grin, "is that I just don't worry so much."

LINDA RONSTADT

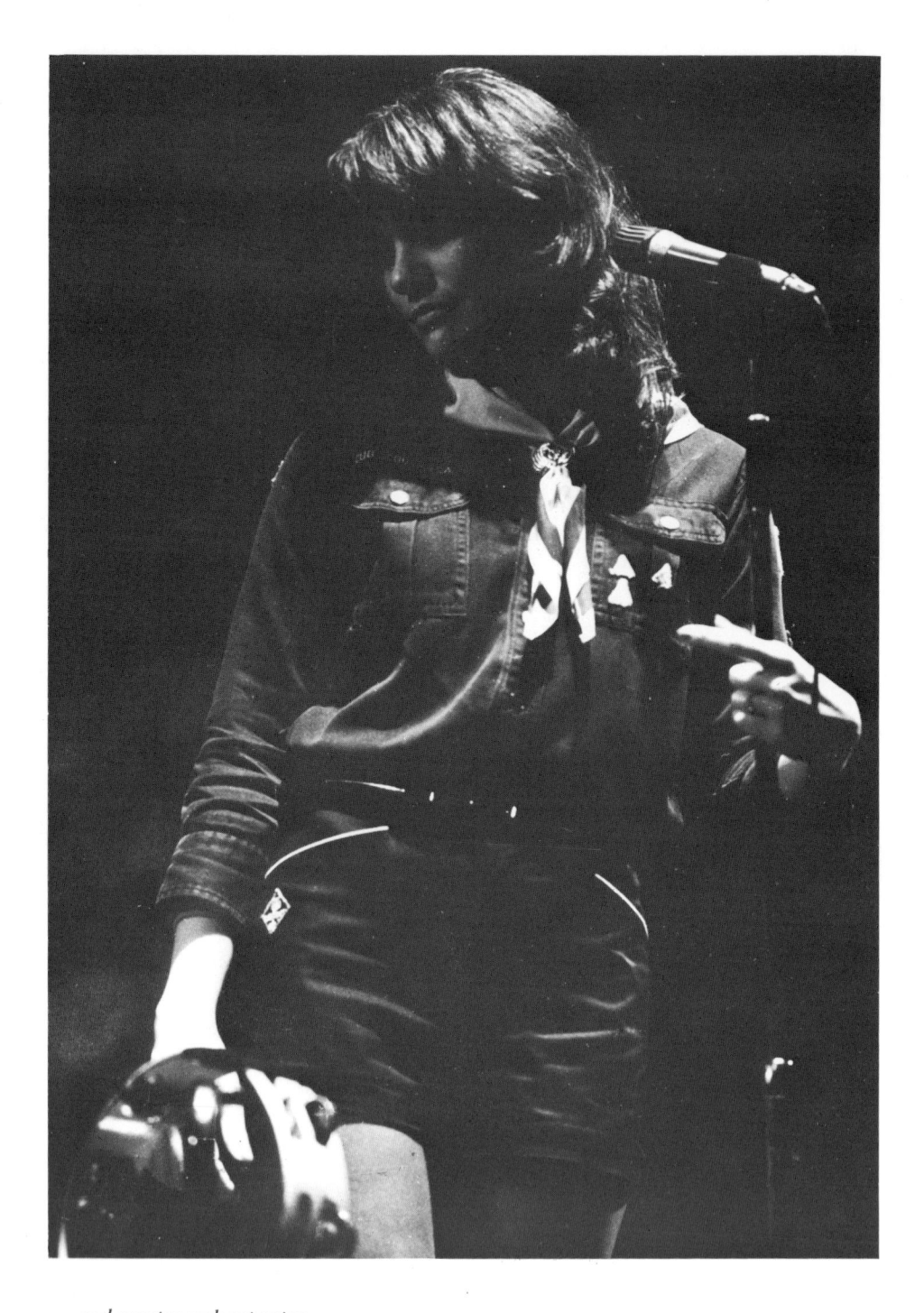

. . . and country-rock superstar.

LINDA RONSTADT DISCOGRAPHY

Albums

THE STONE PONEYS

The Stone Poneys Capitol
Evergreen, Vol. I, Capitol
Evergreen, Vol. II, Capitol

LINDA RONSTADT

Different Drum—Capitol
Hand Sown, Home Grown—Capitol
Linda Ronstadt—Capitol
Don't Cry Now—Capitol
Heart Like A Wheel—Asylum
Greatest Hits—Asylum
Hasten Down The Wind—Asylum
Living in the U.S.A.—Asylum
Prisoner in Disguise—Asylum
Retrospective—Capitol
Silk Purse—Capital
Simple Dreams—Asylum

Singles

THE STONE PONEYS

"Different Drum"—Capitol

LINDA RONSTADT

"Back in the U.S.A."/"White Rhythm and Blues"—Asylum
"Blowing Away"/"Ooh Baby, Baby"—Asylum
"Blue Bayou"/"Old Paint"—Asylum
"Crazy"/"Someone To Lay Down Beside Me"—Asylum
"Heat Wave"/"Tracks of My Tears"—Elektra
"I Never Will Marry"/"Tumbling Dice—Elektra
"Lago Azul"/"Lo Siento Mi Vida"—Asylum
"Long Long Time"—Capitol
"Lose Again"—Asylum
"Love Has No Pride"/"Silver Threads and Golden Needles"—Elektra
"Poor, Poor Pitiful Me"/"Simple Man, Simple Dream"—Asylum
"That'll Be The Day"/"Try Me Again"—Asylum
"When Will I Be Loved"/"You're No Good"—Capitol